BENCHLEY

BESIDE HIMSELF

Books by

ROBERT BENCHLEY

BENCHLEY BESIDE HIMSELF

INSIDE BENCHLEY

AFTER 1903—WHAT?

MY TEN YEARS IN A QUANDARY,
AND HOW THEY GREW

FROM BED TO WORSE: OR COMFORTING
THOUGHTS ABOUT THE BISON

NO POEMS: OR AROUND THE WORLD
BACKWARDS AND SIDEWAYS

PLUCK AND LUCK

THE TREASURER'S REPORT, AND OTHER
ASPECTS OF COMMUNITY SINGING

20,000 LEAGUES UNDER THE SEA, OR
DAVID COPPERFIELD

THE EARLY WORM

LOVE CONQUERS ALL

OF ALL THINGS

BENCHLEY
BESIDE
HIMSELF

by
ROBERT
BENCHLEY

With Drawings by
Gluyas Williams

Harper & Brothers . New York and London

4 - 43

SIXTH EDITION

I-S

**This book is complete and unabridged
in contents, and is manufactured in strict
conformity with Government regulations
for saving paper.**

Table of Contents

Polyp with a Past	1
The Young Idea's Shooting Gallery	4
Open Bookcases	10
How to Sell Goods	15
When Not in Rome Why Do As the Romans Did?	21
African Sculpture	26
"In This Corner—"	33
"I Am in the Book"	40
Hockey Tonight!	50
A Good Old-Fashioned Christmas	57
The New Wing	70
When Genius Remained Your Humble Servant	75
Shakespeare Explained	87
Gardening Notes	91
The Passing of the Orthodox Paradox	98
The Church Supper	103
Horse-Sense Editorial	110
Chemists' Sporting Extra!	112
How Much Does the Sun Jump	116
Looking Shakespeare Over	119
Evolution Sidelights	124
Teaching the Old Idea to Skate	127
Cleaning Out the Desk	131
Carnival Week in Sunny Las Los	138
Another Uncle Edith Christmas Story	146
Community Singing	153
"Go Down, Sweet Jordan"	161
"One Minute, Please"	166
The Mystery of Bridge-Building	173
"They're Off!"	180
Bringing Back the Morris Dance	187

v

The Treasurer's Report   193
The Homelike Hotel   200
The Sunday Menace   209
One Set of French Dishes   218
A Dark Horse in British Sports   223
The Stranger Within Our Gates   230
One-Two-Three-Four   237
Ask Me a Question   245
The King's English   252
Eight O'Clock Sharp   259
Penguin Psychology   264
Now That You're Tanned—What   271
Sporting Life in America: Dozing   277
The Bathroom Revolution   285
What Shall We Say   294
A Vanishing Art   298

ILLUSTRATIONS

*The illustrations, grouped as a separate
section, will be found facing page 150*

Big Executive

Easy Does It

Trying On for Size

One . . . Two . . . Three . . . Bend!

Self-assurance

Position No. 6. Escapist

Mens Sana in Corpore Sano

Anti-social

Frustration

Do Not Disturb

The Midnight Snack

The Football Fan

Easy Two Hands or The Man Doesn't Know His
Own Strength

Le Demi-Penseur

"Yours of the 18th inst. received and contents
noted"

"I'll be down in just a minute!"

BENCHLEY
BESIDE HIMSELF

Polyp with a Past

The Story of an Organism With a Heart

O F ALL forms of animal life, the polyp is probably
the most neglected by fanciers. People seem willing to pay attention to anything, cats, lizards, canaries,
or even fish, but simply because the polyp is reserved by
nature and not given to showing off or wearing its heart
on its sleeve, it is left alone under the sea to slave away
at coral-building with never a kind word or a pat on the
tentacles from anybody.

It was quite by accident that I was brought face to
face with the human side of a polyp. I had been working on a thesis on "Emotional Crises in Sponge Life,"
and came upon a polyp formation on a piece of coral
in the course of my laboratory work. To say that I was
astounded would be putting it mildly. I was surprised.

The difficulty in research work in this field came in
isolating a single polyp from the rest in order to study
the personal peculiarities of the little organism, for, as
is so often the case (even, I fear, with us great big
humans sometimes), the individual behaves in an
entirely different manner in private from the one he
adopts when there is a crowd around. And a polyp,
among all creatures, has a minimum of time to himself
in which to sit down and think. There is always a crowd
of other polyps dropping in on him, urging him to make
a fourth in a string of coral beads or just to come out

1

and stick around on a rock for the sake of good-fellowship.

The one which I finally succeeded in isolating was an engaging organism with a provocative manner and a little way of wrinkling up its ectoderm which put you at once at your ease. There could be no formality about your relations with this polyp five minutes after your first meeting. You were just like one great big family.

Although I have no desire to retail gossip, I think that readers of this treatise ought to be made aware of the fact (if, indeed, they do not already know it) that a polyp is really neither one thing nor another in matters of gender. One day it may be a little boy polyp, another day a little girl, according to its whim or practical considerations of policy. On gray days, when everything seems to be going wrong, it may decide that it will be neither boy nor girl but will just drift. I think that if we big human cousins of the little polyp were to follow the example set by these lowliest of God's creatures in this matter, we all would find ourselves much better off in the end. Am I not right, little polyp?

What was my surprise, then, to discover my little friend one day in a gloomy and morose mood. It refused the peanut-butter which I had brought it and I observed through the microscope that it was shaking with sobs. Lifting it up with a pair of pincers I took it over to the window to let it watch the automobiles go by, a diversion which had, in the past, never failed to amuse. But I could see that it was not interested. A tune from the Victrola fell equally flat, even though I set my little charge on the center of the disc and allowed it to revolve at a dizzy pace, which frolic usually sent it into spasms

2

of excited giggling. Something was wrong. It was under emotional stress of the most racking kind.

I consulted Klunzinger's "Die Korallenthiere des Rothen Meeres" and there found that at an early age the polyp is quite likely to become the victim of a sentimental passion which is directed at its own self.

In other words, my tiny companion was in love with itself, bitterly, desperately, head-over-heels in love.

In an attempt to divert it from this madness, I took it on an extended tour of the Continent, visiting all the old cathedrals and stopping at none but the best hotels. The malady grew worse, instead of better. I thought that perhaps the warm sun of Granada would bring the color back into those pale tentacles, but there the inevitable romance in the soft air was only fuel to the flame, and, in the shadow of the Alhambra, my little polyp gave up the fight and died of a broken heart without ever having declared its love to itself.

I returned to America shortly after not a little chastened by what I had witnessed of Nature's wonders in the realm of passion.

The Young Idea's Shooting Gallery

SINCE we were determined to have Junior edu-cated according to modern methods of child train-ing, a year and a half did not seem too early an age at which to begin. As Doris said: "There is no reason why a child of a year and a half shouldn't have rudimentary cravings for self-expression." And really, there isn't any reason, when you come right down to it.

Doris had been reading books on the subject, and had been talking with Mrs. Deemster. Most of the trouble in our town can be traced back to someone's having been talking with Mrs. Deemster. Mrs. Deemster brings an evangelical note into the simplest social conversations, so that by the time your wife is through the second piece of cinnamon toast she is convinced that all children should have their knee-pants removed before they are four, or that you should hire four servants a day on three-hour shifts, or that, as in the present case, no child should be sent to a regular school until he has deter-mined for himself what his profession is going to be and then should be sent straight from the home to Johns Hopkins or the Sorbonne.

Junior was to be left entirely to himself, the theory being that he would find self-expression in some form or other, and that by watching him carefully it could be determined just what should be developed in him, or, rather, just what he should be allowed to develop in himself. He was not to be corrected in any way, or

4

guided, and he was to call us "Doris" and "Monty" instead of "Mother" and "Father." We were to be just pals, nothing more. Otherwise, his individuality would become submerged. I was, however, to be allowed to pay what few bills he might incur until he should find himself.

The first month that Junior was "on his own," striving for self-expression, he spent practically every waking hour of each day in picking the mortar out from between the bricks in the fire-place and eating it.

"Don't you think you ought to suggest to him that nobody who really *is* anybody eats mortar?" I said.

"I don't like to interfere," replied Doris. "I'm trying to figure out what it may mean. He may have the makings of a sculptor in him." But one could see that she was a little worried, so I didn't say the cheap and obvious thing, that at any rate he had the makings of a sculptor in him or would have in a few more days of self-expression.

Soft putty was put at his disposal, in case he might feel like doing a little modeling. We didn't expect much of him at first, of course; maybe just a panther or a little General Sherman; but if that was to be his *métier* we weren't going to have it said that his career was nipped in the bud for the lack of a little putty.

The first thing that he did was to stop up the key-hole in the bath-room door while I was in the tub, so that I had to crawl out on the piazza roof and into the guest-room window. It did seem as if there might be some way of preventing a recurrence of that sort of thing without submerging his individuality too much.

5

But Doris said no. If he were disciplined now, he would grow up nursing a complex against putty and against me and might even try to marry Aunt Marian. She had read of a little boy who had been punished by his father for putting soap on the cellar stairs, and from that time on, all the rest of his life, every time he saw soap he went to bed and dreamed that he was riding in the cab of a runaway engine dressed as Perriot, which meant, of course, that he had a suppressed desire to kill his father.

It almost seemed, however, as if the risk were worth taking if Junior could be shown the fundamentally anti-social nature of an act like stuffing keyholes with putty, but nothing was done about it except to take the putty supply away for that day.

The chief trouble came, however, in Junior's contacts with other neighborhood children whose parents had not seen the light. When Junior would lead a movement among the young bloods to pull up the Hemmings' nasturtiums or would show flashes of personality by hitting little Leda Hemming over the forehead with a trowel, Mrs. Hemming could never be made to see that to reprimand Junior would be to crush out his God-given individuality. All she would say was, "Just look at those nasturtiums!" over and over again. And the Hemming children were given to understand that it would be all right if they didn't play with Junior quite so much.

This morning, however, the thing solved itself. While expressing himself in putty in the nursery, Junior succeeded in making a really excellent life-mask of Mrs.

6

Mrs. Deemster didn't enter into the spirit of the thing at all

Deemster's fourteen-months-old little girl who had come over to spend the morning with him. She had a little difficulty in breathing, but it really was a fine mask. Mrs. Deemster, however, didn't enter into the spirit of the thing at all, and after excavating her little girl, took Doris aside. It was decided that Junior is perhaps too young to start in on his career unguided.

That is Junior that you can hear now, I think.

Open Bookcases

THINGS have come to a pretty pass when a man can't buy a bookcase that hasn't got glass doors on it. What are we becoming—a nation of weaklings?

All over New York city I have been—trying to get something in which to keep books. And what am I shown? Curio cabinets, inclosed whatnots, museum cases in which to display fragments from the neolithic age, and glass-faced sarcophagi for dead butterflies.

"But I am apt to use my books at any time," I explain to the salesman. "I never can tell when it is coming on me. And when I want a book I want it quickly. I don't want to have to send down to the office for the key, and I don't want to have to manipulate any trick ball-bearings and open up a case as if I were getting cream-puffs out for a customer. I want a bookcase for books and not books for a bookcase."

(I really don't say all those clever things to the clerk. It took me quite a while to think them up. What I really say is, timidly, "Haven't you any bookcases without glass doors?" and when they say "No," I thank them and walk into the nearest dining-room table.)

But if they keep on getting arrogant about it I shall speak up to them one of these fine days. When I ask for an open-faced bookcase they look with a scornful smile across the salesroom toward the mahogany four-posters and say:

I thank them and walk into the nearest dining-room table

"Oh, no, we don't carry those any more. We don't have any call for them. Every one uses the glass-doored ones now. They keep the books much cleaner."

Then the ideal procedure for a real book-lover would be to keep his books in the original box, snugly packed in excelsior, with the lid nailed down. Then they would be nice and clean. And the sun couldn't get at them and ruin the bindings. Faugh! (Try saying that. It doesn't work out at all as you think it's going to. And it makes you feel very silly for having tried it.)

Why, in the elder days bookcases with glass doors were owned only by people who filled them with ten volumes of a pictorial history of the Civil War (including some swell steel engravings) , "Walks and Talks with John L. Stoddard" and "Daily Thoughts for Daily Needs," done in robin's-egg blue with a watered silk bookmark dangling out. A set of Sir Walter Scott always helps fill out a bookcase with glass doors. It looks well from the front and shows that you know good literature when you see it. And you don't have to keep opening and shutting the doors to get it out, for you never want to get it out.

A bookcase with glass doors used to be a sign that somewhere in the room there was a crayon portrait of Father when he was a young man, with a real piece of glass stuck on the portrait to represent a diamond stud.

And now we are told that "every one buys book-cases with glass doors; we have no call for others." Soon we shall be told that the thing to do is to buy the false backs of bindings, such as they have in stage libraries, to string across behind the glass. It will keep us from read-

13

ing too much, and then, too, no one will want to borrow our books.

But one clerk told me the truth. And I am just fearless enough to tell it here. I know that it will kill my chances for the Presidency, but I cannot stop to think of that.

After advising me to have a carpenter build me the kind of bookcase I wanted, and after I had told him that I had my name in for a carpenter but wasn't due to get him until late in the fall, as he was waiting for prices to go higher before taking the job on, the clerk said:

"That's it. It's the price. You see the furniture manufacturers can make much more money out of a bookcase with glass doors than they can without. When by hanging glass doors on a piece of furniture at but little more expense to themselves they can get a much bigger profit, what's the sense in making them without glass doors? They have just stopped making them, that's all."

So you see the American people are being practically forced into buying glass doors whether they want them or not. Is that right? Is it fair? Where is our personal liberty going to? What is becoming of our traditional American institutions?

I don't know.

How to Sell Goods

THE Retail Merchants' Association ought to buy up all the copies of "Elements of Retail Salesmanship," by Paul Westley Ivey (Macmillan), and not let a single one get into the hands of a customer, for once the buying public reads what is written there the game is up. It tells all about how to sell goods to people, how to appeal to their weaknesses, how to exert subtle influences which will win them over in spite of themselves. Houdini might as well issue a pamphlet giving in detail his methods of escape as for the merchants of this country to let this book remain in circulation.

The art of salesmanship is founded, according to Mr. Ivey, on, first, a thorough knowledge of the goods which are to be sold, and second, a knowledge of the customer. By knowing the customer you know what line of argument will most appeal to him. There are several lines in popular use. First is the appeal to the instinct of self-preservation—i.e., social self-preservation. The customer is made to feel that in order to preserve her social standing she must buy the article in question. "She must be made to feel what a disparaged social self would mean to her mental comfort."

It is reassuring to know that it is a recognized ruse on the part of the salesman to intimate that unless you buy a particular article you will have to totter through life branded as the arch-piker. I have always taken this atti-

15

tude of the clerks perfectly seriously. In fact, I have worried quite a bit about it.

In the store where I am allowed to buy my clothes it is quite the thing among the salesmen to see which one of them can degrade me most. They intimate that, while they have no legal means of refusing to sell their goods to me, it really would be much more in keeping with things if I were to take the few pennies that I have at my disposal and run around the corner to some little haberdashery for my shirts and ties. Every time I come out from that store I feel like Ethel Barrymore in "Déclassée." Much worse, in fact, for I haven't any good looks to fall back upon.

But now that I know the clerks are simply acting all that scorn in an attempt to appeal to my instinct for the preservation of my social self, I can face them without flinching. When that pompous old boy with the sandy mustache who has always looked upon me as a member of the degenerate Juke family tries to tell me that if I don't take the five-dollar cravat he won't be responsible for the way in which decent people will receive me when I go out on the street, I will reach across the counter and playfully pull his own necktie out from his waistcoat and scream, "I know you, you old rascal! You got that stuff from page 68 of 'Elements of Retail Salesmanship' (Macmillan)."

Other traits which a salesperson may appeal to in the customer are: Vanity, parental pride, greed, imitation, curiosity and selfishness. One really gets in touch with a lot of nice people in this work and can bring out the very best that is in them.

Customers are divided into groups indicative of tem-

16

They intimate that I had better take my few pennies and run 'round the corner to some little haberdashery

perament. There is first the Impulsive or Nervous Customer. She is easily recognized because she walks into the store in "a quick, sometimes jerky manner. Her eyes are keen-looking; her expression is intense, oftentimes appearing strained." She must be approached promptly, according to the book, and what she desires must be quickly ascertained. Since these are the rules for selling to people who enter the store in this manner, it might be well, no matter how lethargic you may be by nature, to assume the appearance of the Impulsive or Nervous Customer as soon as you enter the store, adopting a quick, even jerky manner and making your eyes as keen-looking as possible, with an intense expression, oftentimes appearing strained. Then the clerk will size you up as type No. 1 and will approach you promptly. After she has quickly filled your order you may drop the impulsive pose and assume your natural, slow manner again, whereupon the clerk will doubtless be highly amused at having been so cleverly fooled into giving quick service.

The opposite type is known as the Deliberate Customer. She walks slowly and in a dignified manner. Her facial expression is calm and poised. "Gestures are uncommon, but if existing tend to be slow and inconspicuous." She can wait.

Then there is the Vacillating or Indecisive Customer, the Confident or Decisive Customer (this one should be treated with subtle flattery and agreement with all her views), the Talkative or Friendly Customer, and the Silent or Indifferent one. All these have their little weaknesses, and the perfect salesperson will learn to know these and play to them.

There seems to be only one thing left for the customer to do in order to meet this concerted attack upon his personality. That is, to hire some expert like Mr. Ivey to study the different types of sales men and women and formulate methods of meeting their offensive. Thus, if I am of the type designated as the Vacillating or Indecisive Customer, I ought to know what to do when confronted by a salesman of the Aristocratic, Scornful type, so that I may not be bulldozed into buying something I do not want.

If I could only find such a book of instructions I would go tomorrow and order a black cotton engineer's shirt from that sandy-mustached salesman and bawl him out if he raised his eyebrows. But not having the book, I shall go in and, without a murmur, buy a $3 silk shirt for $18 and slink out feeling that if I had been any kind of sport at all I would also have bought that cork helmet in the showcase.

When Not in Rome, Why Do As the Romans Did?

THERE is a growing sentiment among sign painters that when a sign or notice is to be put up in a public place it should be written in characters that are at least legible, so that, to quote "The Manchester Guardian" (as every one seems to do) "He who runs may read."

This does not strike one as being an unseemly pandering to popular favor. The supposition is that the sign is put there to be read, otherwise it would have been turned over to an inmate of the Odd Fellows Home to be engraved on the head of a pin. And what could be a more fair requirement than that it should be readable?

Advertising, with its billboard message of rustless screens and co-educational turkish-baths, has done much to further the good cause, and a glance through the files of newspapers of seventy-five years ago, when the big news story of the day was played up in diamond type easily deciphered in a strong light with the naked eye, shows that news printing has not, to use a slang phrase, stood still.

But in the midst of this uniform progress we find a stagnant spot. Surrounded by legends that are patent and easy to read and understand, we find the stone-cutter and the architect still putting up tablets and corner-stones, monuments and cornices, with dates disguised in Roman numerals. It is as if it were a game, in which they

21

were saying, "The number we are thinking of is even; it begins with M; it has five digits and when they are spread out, end to end, they occupy three feet of space. You have until we count to one hundred to guess what it is."

Roman numerals are all right for a rainy Sunday afternoon or to take a convalescent's mind from his illness, but to put them in a public place, where the reader stands a good chance of being run over by a dray if he spends more than fifty seconds in their perusal, is not in keeping with the efficiency of the age. If for no other reason than the extra space they take, involving more marble, more of the cutter's time and wear and tear on his instruments, not to mention the big overhead, you would think that Roman numerals would have been abolished long ago.

Of course, they can be figured out if you're good at that sort of thing. By working on your cuff and backs of envelopes, you can translate them in no time at all compared to the time taken by a cocoon to change into a butterfly, for instance. All you have to do is remember that "M" stands for either "*millium*," meaning thousand, or for "million." By referring to the context you can tell which is more probable. If, for example, it is a date, you can tell right away that it doesn't mean "million," for there isn't any "million" in our dates. And there is one-seventh or eighth of your number deciphered already. Then "C," of course, stands for "*centum*," which you can translate by working backwards at it, taking such a word as "century" or "per cent," and looking up what they come from, and there you have it! By this time it is hardly the middle of the afternoon, and all you have before you is a combination of X's, I's and an L, the latter standing for "Elevated Railway," and "Licorice," or, if you cross it with two little horizontal lines, it stands for the English pound, which is equivalent to about four dollars and eighty-odd cents in real money. Simple as sawing through a log.

But it takes time. That's the big trouble with it. You can't do the right thing by the office and go in for Roman numerals, too. And since most of the people who pass such inscriptions are dependent on their own earnings, why not cater to them a bit and let them in on the secret?

Probably the only reason that the people haven't risen up and demanded a reform along these lines is because so few of them really give a hang what the inscription says. If the American Antiquarian Turn-Verein doesn't care about stating in understandable figures the date on which the cornerstone of their building was laid, the average citizen is perfectly willing to let the matter drop right there.

But it would never do to revert to Roman numerals in, say, the arrangement of time-tables. How long would the commuter stand it if he had to mumble to himself for twenty minutes and use up the margins of his newspaper before he could figure out what was the next train after the 5:18? Or this, over the telephone between wife and husband:

"Hello, dear! I think I'll come in town for lunch. What trains can I get?"

"Just a minute—I'll look them up. Hold the wire. . . . Let's see, here's one at XII:LVIII, that's twelve, and L is a thousand and V is five and three I's are three; that

23

makes 12: one thousand. . . . that can't be right. . . .
now XII certainly is twelve, and L . . . what does L stand
for? . . . I say, what—does—L—stand—for? . . . Well,
ask Helma. . . . What does she say? . . . Fifty? . . . Sure,
that makes it come out all right. . . . 12:58. . . . What time
is it now? . . . 1 o'clock? . . . Well, the next one leaves
Oakam at I:XLIV. . . . that's . . ." etc.

Batting averages and the standing of teams in the
leagues are another department where the introduction
of Roman numerals would be suicide for the political
party in power at the time. For of all things that are essential to the day's work of the voter, an early enlighten-
ment in the matter of the home team's standing and
the numerical progress of the favorite batsman are of
primary importance. This information has to be gleaned
on the way to work in the morning, and, except for those
who come in to work each day from North Philadelphia
or the Croton Reservoir, it would be a physical impos-
sibility to figure the tables out and get any of the day's
news besides.

CLVB BATTING RECORDS

	Games	At Bat	Runs	B.H.	S.B.	S.H.	Aver.
Detroit	CLII	MMMMXXCIX	DCLIII	MCCCXXXIII	CLXVIII	CC	CCLXII
Chicago	CLI	MMMMCMXL	DLXXI	MCCXLVI	CLXXIX	CCXXI	CCLII
Cleveland	CLII	MMMMCMXXXVII	DCXIX	MCCXXXI	CL	CCXXI	CCXLIX
Boston	CLI	MMMMDCCCLXXIV	DXXXIV	MCXCI	CXXXVI	CCXXV	CCXLV
New York	CL	MMMMCMLXXXVII	DLIV	MCCXXX	CLXXV	CLXV	CCXLVII
Washington	CLIII	MMMMCMXXXVIII	DV	MCXC	CLXIII	CLXV	CCXDI
St. Louis	CLV	MMMMMLXV	DLXXIV	MCCXXI	CCVII	CLXII	CCXLI
Philadelphia	CXLIX	MMMMDCCCXXVI	CCCCXVI	MCXLIII	CXLIII	CLV	CCXXXVII

You can't do right by the office and go in for
roman numerals too

On matters such as these the proletariat would have
protested the Roman numeral long ago. If they are will-

ing to let its reactionary use on tablets and monuments stand it is because of their indifference to influences which do not directly affect their pocketbooks. But if it could be put up to them in a powerful cartoon, showing the Architect and the Stone-Cutter dressed in frock coats and silk hats, with their pockets full of money, stepping on the Common People so that he cannot see what is written on the tablet behind them, then perhaps the public would realize how they are being imposed on.

For that there is an organized movement among architects and stone-cutters to keep these things from the citizenry there can no longer be any doubt. It is not only a matter of the Roman numerals. How about the use of the "V" when "U" should be used? You will always see it in inscriptions. "SVMNER BVILDING" is one of the least offensive. Perhaps the excuse is that "V" is more adapted to stone-lettering. Then why not carry this principle out further? Why not use the letter H when S is meant? Or substitute K for B? If the idea is to deceive, and to make it easier for the stone-cutter, a pleasing effect could be got from the inscription, "Erected in 1897 by the Society of Arts and Grafts," by making it read: "EKEATEW IZ MXIXLXIXLXXII LY THE XNLIEZY OF AEXA ZNL ELAFTX." There you have letters that are all adapted to stone-cutting; they look well together, and they are, in toto, as intelligible as most inscriptions.

African Sculpture

Its Background, Future and the Old-Fashioned Waltz

(With Photographs by the Author)

A RECENT exhibition of West African sculpture created a furor in art circles which died down in about fifteen minutes—which was just about the time consumed in removing the *objects* from the packing crates. We are therefore printing a critical estimate of these little carvings in an attempt to arouse enough interest in them among art lovers to have them crated up again to be sent back to West Africa.

One must understand the spirit which is at the back of West African sculpture in order to appreciate the intense *integrity* of its technique. It isn't so much the sculpture itself (although, in a way, it *is*) as the fact that it is filled with raisins. These can be extracted and eaten if you like raisins. Early Florentine sculpture and late Greek modeling (some of the late Greek was so late that it ran right over into Early Florentine and nobody knew the difference) had no raisins.

A study of the examples printed on this page will hardly serve to demonstrate this point, but it won't do any harm to look at them casually.

Example 1 is a native West African funeral mask, worn by any relative of the deceased who wanted to attend the funeral and yet didn't want the rest of the relatives to know that he was in town. This would prob-

Funeral mask worn by relatives who want to look Irish

West African salt-cellar fetish, showing the growth of grain from the seedling to the ripe kernel

ably account for the strong Irish cast to the features of the mask. No one would think of an Irishman being a relative of a native West African, although stranger things *have* happened. This mask was brought back by the Huber's 42nd St. Museum expedition and is now on exhibition in the Renaissance Biped Room of the Museum itself.

Example 2 is one of the most sincere of these native sculptures. It is a local fetish in the shape of a salt-cellar (a pretty funny shape for a salt-cellar, you are doubtless saying to yourself), as salt is considered to be very lucky on the West Coast of Africa, especially if you happen to have any fried chicken and hashed-in-cream potatoes to put it on. This salt-cellar fetish, in addition to being a talisman, also tells a story (stop it if you have heard it):

It represents the gradual growth of the seed to the mature plant, the seed being represented by the two hands of the little figure and the mature plant by the two knees. In the spring of the year, when the seed is planted, everything is bright and green. Hence the hands. In the fall, when the grain is garnered, the year is nearing its close, Nature is putting on her winding sheet for the long winter, and nothing seems right. Hence the knees. That may not be the explanation at all. How should *I* know?

Example 3 is a poser, frankly. It was found on the West Coast, in a district known as the "West Coast Studios." Nobody seems to know who found this example of native art, or where it was found. It just turned up among some other bits of sculpture in the Museum's shipment. At first it was thought to be a bust of the local Lon Cha . . . Beg pardon! At first it was thought to be

31

a replica of Naa, the Fog-God—and it still may be. The argument against this theory is that it isn't round

This doesn't seem to mean much to any one

enough. Other experts have placed it in the Post-Fever School (after the scourge of fever which swept the Coast in 1780) and seem to see in it an attempt to show the growth of the seed to the mature grain. Here, again, finders are keepers.

Now, a study of these three examples, representing, as they do, three distinct schools of West African sculptural art, shows us one thing—namely, that long before the coming of the White Man there was a distinct feeling for æsthetic expression among the natives of that section of the continent. Just how successful these savage strivings were, and just what degree of skill was mastered by these tribal artists, is something which each connoisseur must decide for himself. Personally, I wouldn't give them houseroom.

"In This Corner—"

FRANKLY, I am not much of a fight fan. I always get sorry for the one who is getting socked. On the other hand, if *no* one is getting socked, I am bored and start screaming for blood. There is no such thing as pleasing me at a fight.

Of course, as I keep saying to myself when I get to worrying over the loser's suffering, he probably expects this sort of thing. When a man decides to be a fighter he must know that sooner or later he is going to get his nose mashed in. He takes that chance. So there is really no need for me to feel so bad about it. God knows, I have troubles enough of my own without sitting and wincing every time some Lithuanian bunker-boy gets punched in the side of the head.

But somehow I can't help feeling that the one who is getting mashed is pretty fairly surprised that things have taken this turn—and not a little mortified. I am afraid that he didn't want to fight in the first place, but was forced into it by his backers. Perhaps, if I read more of the fighters' statements before the fight, I would feel a little less sorry for them when I hear their faces give way. Once I read what a welterweight said on the day before the contest, and, for the first time, I actually enjoyed seeing his lip swell up.

Probably my tender feelings in the matter are due to an instinctive habit I have of putting myself in the

33

place of anyone I am watching. I haven't been at a fight for more than three minutes before I begin indulging in one of my favorite nightmares. This consists of imagining that I myself am up in the ring facing the better of the two men.

Just how I am supposed to have got up in the ring is never quite clear. I don't believe that I ever would sign up deliberately for a prize fight, much as I need the money. I can think of at least fourteen thousand things that I would try first. But the idea seems to be that while drugged or under the influence of alcohol I have agreed to meet some prominent pugilist in the Yankee Stadium and, quite naturally, the affair has filled the mammoth bowl with a record crowd, all of whom are cynically antagonistic to me.

Whatever my mental processes may have been which led me to don silken tights and crawl through the ropes, my reverie begins when I awake to find myself standing under the terrific glare of the lights going through the formality of shaking gloves with a very large man.

"Here, here, Benchley," I say to myself. "What's all this? This is a very foolhardy thing to be doing."

But there is no way of backing out now and the only thing that I can do is to throw a big bluff that I know something about boxing.

Now, as a matter of fact, my fighting technique is limited to a few elementary passes learned in a gymnasium class when I was in school, and consists of a rather trusting stance with the arms raised as if posing for a photograph, followed by a quick lunge forward with my left and an almost simultaneous jump backward. The fact

34

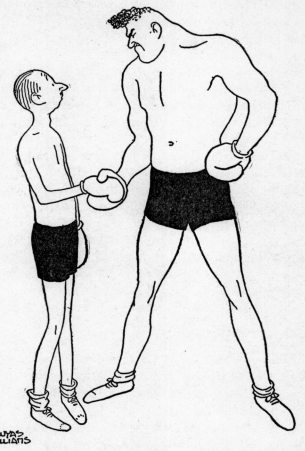

"Here, here, Benchley," I say to myself. "This is a very foolhardy thing to be doing"

that this is all done to a count, "one, two, three, and four," leaves something to be desired as strategy. I also have a nasty right hook—done to "five, six, seven, and eight"—which, I think, would deceive no one. I have tried both of these on the younger of my two boys, and he found little difficulty in solving them the very first time. Fortunately, I had the reach, however.

Equipped with these two primary attacks, each of which resolves itself into the quick jump backward, I am supposed to pit myself against a trained fighter. The whole thing is pretty terrifying to start with and rapidly grows worse.

The trouble with my position No. 1 seems to be that my opponent doesn't wait for me. No sooner have I taken my stance and raised my fists than I am the recipient of a terrific clout on the ear, without even the formality of counting "one, two, three, and four." Without seeing very much of anything at the time, I try my left hook, which ends very badly somewhere in midair, and again take a rapid succession of neck-bending socks on either side of the jaw. At this juncture, I decide to lie down.

This strategy on my part is greeted with derisive hoots from the crowd, but there seems to be nothing else to be done about it. There is practically nothing that my opponent can't do to me and nobody knows it better than I do. Furthermore, I am not one of those people who develop a gameness under physical pain. I am not a glutton for punishment. If I had my way about it I would practically *never* let myself be hurt. In the waiting room of a dentist's office I have been known to develop a yellow streak which is clearly visible through my clothing. Gameness is a grand quality and it is all right as a last resort, but my motto is "Try everything else first."

Consequently, in the position in which I now find myself, my first thought is how to get out of the ring and into bed with the covers pulled over my head. I try crawling out through the ropes, but in this particular dream-fight of mine, there is a rule against throwing in the towel. Both fighters must go the entire fifteen rounds, dead or alive. So you can see my predicament.

I very seldom get much farther than this point in my reverie. I suppose that I would just lie there on the floor and make my opponent come to me if he wanted to hit me. I am very certain that I would not be fool enough to get up on my feet again. I might try kicking him in the shins from my recumbent position, but I doubt that I would bring myself to even that show of belligerence. I would simply have to trust in his seeing the humor of the thing and good-naturedly getting down on the floor beside me and wrestling the rest of the fight out. He would win that, too, but I wouldn't get those socks on the side of the head at any rate.

As I snap out of this dream state and find myself sitting in my safe ringside seat (from which I can see nothing, owing to the holders of ringside seats in front of me indulging in the good American custom of standing up whenever things get interesting) my first sensation is one of great relief at my good fortune in not being in the ring. But then I see some other poor son-of-a-gun getting what I might have had, and I can't help but wish that the whole thing would stop. Maybe he, too, found himself up there quite by accident.

Of course, there is one thing about prize fights that one sees nowadays. In a large majority of them no one gets hurt enough even to *want* to stop before it is over. Sometimes it is hard to tell who is the winner, and the most serious injury sustained by either fighter is a little skin rubbed off the inside of his arms from waltzing. At least, I have the distinction of having taken part in the most brutal fight of modern times.

"I Am in the Book"

THERE are several natural phenomena which I shall have to have explained to me before I can consent to keep on going as a resident member of the human race. One is the metamorphosis which hats and suits undergo exactly one week after their purchase, whereby they are changed from smart, intensely becoming articles of apparel into something children use when they want to "dress up like daddy." Another is the almost identical change undergone by people whom you have known under one set of conditions when they are transferred to another locale.

Perhaps the first phenomenon, in my case, may be explained by the fact that I need a valet. Not a valet to come in two or three times a week and sneak my clothes away, but a valet to follow me about, everywhere I go, with a whiskbroom in one hand and an electric iron in the other, brushing off a bit of lint here, giving an occasional *coup de fer* there, and whispering in my ear every once in a while, for God's sake not to turn my hat brim down that way. Then perhaps my hats and suits would remain the hats and suits they were when I bought them.

But the second mysterious transformation—that of people of one sort into people of another sort, simply by moving them from one place to another in different clothes—here is a problem for the scientists; that is, if they are at all interested.

40

I need a valet to follow me about, everywhere I go

Perhaps I do not make myself clear. (I have had quite
a bit of trouble that way lately.) I will give an example
if you can get ten other people to give, too. Let us say
that you went to Europe one summer. You were that
rosy-faced man in a straw hat who went to Europe. Or
you went to the seashore. My God, man, you must
have gone *somewhere!*

Before long you were exchanging bits of fruit from your baskets

Wherever you were, you made new acquaintances,
unless you had whooping cough all the time. On the
voyage home, let us say, you sat next to some awfully
nice people from Grand Rapids, or were ill at practically
the same time as a very congenial man from Philadelphia. These chance acquaintances ripened into friend-
ships, and perhaps into something even more beautiful
(although I often think that *nothing* is really more beautiful than friendship) , and before long you were talking
over all kinds of things and perhaps exchanging bits of
fruit from your steamer baskets. By the day before you

43

landed you were practically brother and sister—or, what is worse, brother and brother.

"Now we must get together in the fall," you say. "I am in the book. The first time you come to town give me a ring and we'll go places and see things." And you promise to do the same thing whenever you happen to be in Grand Rapids or Philadelphia. You even think that you might make a trip to Grand Rapids or Philadelphia especially to stage a get-together.

The first inkling you have that maybe you won't quite take a trip to Grand Rapids or Philadelphia is on the day when you land in New York. That morning everyone appears on deck dressed in traveling clothes which they haven't worn since they got on board. They may be very nice clothes and you may all look very smart, but something is different. A strange tenseness has sprung up and everyone walks around the deck trying to act natural, without any more success than seeming singularly unattractive. Some of your bosom friends, with whom you have practically been on the floor of the bar all the way over, you don't even recognize in their civilian clothes. "Why, look who's here!" you say. "It's Eddie! I didn't know you, Eddie, with that great, big, beautiful collar on." And Eddie asks you where you got that hat, accompanying the question with a playful jab in the ribs which doesn't quite come off. A rift has already appeared in the lute and you haven't even been examined yet by the doctors for trachoma.

By the time you get on the dock and are standing around among the trunks and dogs, you may catch sight of those darling people, the Dibbles, standing in the next section under "C," and you wave weakly and call out, "Don't forget, I'm in the book!" but you know in your heart that you could be in a book of French drawings and the Dibbles wouldn't look you up—which is O. K. with you.

Sometimes, however, they do look you up. Perhaps you have parted at the beach on a bright morning in September before you went up to get dressed for the trip to the city. The Durkinses (dear old Durkinses!) were lying around in their bathing suits and you were just out from your last swim preparatory to getting into the blue suit.

"Well, you old sons-of-guns," you say, smiling through your tears, "the minute you hit town give us a ring and we'll begin right where we left off. I know a good place. We can't swim there, but, boy, we can get wet!"

At which Mr. and Mrs. Durkins scream with laughter and report to Mr. and Mrs. Weffer, who are sitting next, that you have said that you know a place in town where you can't swim but, boy, you can get wet. This pleases the Weffers, too, and they are included in the invitation.

"We'll have a regular Throg's Point reunion," Mrs. Weffer says. Mrs. Weffer isn't so hot at making wisecracks, but she has a good heart. Sure, bring her along!

Along about October you come into the office and find that a Mr. Durkins has called and wants you to call him at his hotel. "Durkins? Durkins? Oh, *Durkins!* Sure thing! Get me Mr. Durkins, please." And a big party is arranged for that night.

At six o'clock you call for the Durkinses at their hotel. (The Weffers have lost interest long before this and dropped out. The Durkinses don't even know where they are—in Montclair, New Jersey, they think.) The

Durkinses are dressed in their traveling clothes and you are in your business suit, such as it is (such as *business* is). You are not quite sure that it *is* Mrs. Durkins at first without that yellow sweater she used to wear all the time at the beach. And Mr. Durkins looks like a house-detective in that collar and tie. They both look ten years older and not very well. You have a feeling that you look pretty seedy, too.

"Well, well, here we are again! How are you all?"

"Fine and dandy. How are you—and the missus?"

"Couldn't be better. She's awfully sorry she couldn't get in town tonight. (You haven't even told her that the Durkinses were here.) What's the news at dear old Throg's Point?"

"Oh, nothing much. Very dead after you left."

"Well, well— (A pause.) How have you *been* anyway, you old son-of-a-gun?"

"Oh, fine; fine and dandy! You all been well?"

"Couldn't be better. What was going on at the old dump when you left? Any news? Any scandal?"

"Not a thing."

"Well, well— Not a thing, eh?— Well, that's the way it goes, you know; that's the way it goes."

"Yes, sir, I guess you're right— You look fine."

"Feel fine—I could use a little swim right now, though."

"Oh, boy, couldn't I though!" (The weather being very cold for October, this is recognized by both sides as an entirely false enthusiasm, as neither of you ever really cared for swimming even in summer.)

"How would you like to take a walk up to Sammy's for a lobster sandwich, eh?"

46

The general atmosphere is that of a meeting in a doctor's office

"Say, what I couldn't do to one right now! *Boy!* Or one of those hot dogs!"

"One of Sammy's hot dogs *wouldn't* go bad right now, you're right."

"Well, well— You've lost all your tan, haven't you?"

"Lost it when I took my first hot-water bath."

This gets a big laugh, the first, and last, of the evening. You are talking to a couple of strangers and the conversation has to be given adrenalin every three minutes to keep it alive. The general atmosphere is that of a meeting in a doctor's office.

It all ends up by your remembering that, after dinner, you have to go to a committee meeting which may be over at nine o'clock or may last until midnight and they had better not wait for you. You will meet them after the theatre if you can. And you know that you can't, and *they* know that you can't, and, what is more, they don't care.

So there you are! The example that I gave has been rather long; so there isn't much room left for a real discussion of the problem. But the fact remains that people are one thing in one place and another thing in another place, just as a hat that you buy in the store for a natty gray sport model turns out to be a Confederate general's fatigue-cap when you get it home. And if you know of any explanation, I don't care to hear about it. I'm sick of the subject by now anyway.

Hockey Tonight!

THE growth of hockey in the brief period which spans my own life is a matter of great interest to me. Sometimes I sit and think about it for hours at a time. "How hockey has grown!" I muse, "How hockey has grown!" And then it is dinner-time and I have done no work.

"I was never very good at it"

But, frankly, hockey is a great big sport now, and I can remember when its only function was to humiliate me personally. I never was very good at it, owing to weak ankles which bent at right angles whenever I started out to skate fast after the puck. I was all right standing still or gliding slowly along, but let me make a spurt and—bendo—out they would go! This made me more or less the butt of the game and I finally gave the whole thing up and took to drinking.

But, at that time, hockey was an informal game, played mostly by small boys with a view to hogging the ice when others, including little girls and myself, wanted to skate. It is true, there was a sort of professional hockey played on an indoor rink at Mechanics' Hall, but that was done on roller skates and was called "polo."

"Polo," as played by the professional teams from Fall River and Providence, was the forerunner of the more intimate maneuvers of the Great War. The players were all state charges out on probation, large men who had given their lives over to some form of violence or other, and the idea was to catch the opposing player with the polo stick as near to the temple as possible and so end the game sooner. A good, livid welt across the cheek was considered a compromise, but counted the striker three points, nevertheless, just to encourage marksmanship. It was estimated that the life of an average indoor polo-player was anywhere from six to eight hours.

Then, gradually, the game of ice-hockey came into ascendancy in the colleges. It was made a major sport in many of them, the players winning their letter for playing in the big games and falling behind in their studies, just as in football and baseball. I was on the student council in my own university when the decision was made to give the members of the hockey team a straight letter without the humiliation of crossed hockey sticks as a bar-sinister as heretofore, and the strain of the debate and momentousness of the question were so great that, after it had all been decided and the letters had been awarded, we all had to go and lie down and rest. Some of us didn't get up again for four or five days. I sometimes wonder if I *ever* got up.

And then came professional hockey as we know it now, with the construction of mammoth rinks and the introduction of frankfurters in the lobbies. Every large city bought itself a hockey team to foster civic spirit, each team composed almost exclusively of Canadians, thereby making the thing a local matter—local to the North American continent, that is.

As at present played, hockey is a fast game, expert and clean, which gives the players plenty of chance to skate very fast from one end of a rink to the other and the spectators a chance to catch that cold in the head they have been looking for. Thousands of people flock to the arenas to witness the progress of the teams in the league and to cheer their fellow townsmen from Canada in their fierce rivalry with players, also from Canada, who wear the colors of Boston, New York, Detroit, and other presumptuous cities. As the number of cities which support hockey teams increases, the difficulty is going to come in impressing on the French-Canadian players the names of the cities they are playing for, so that they won't get mixed up in the middle of the game and start working for the wrong side. A Frenchman playing for Chillicothe or Amagansett will have to watch himself pretty carefully.

However, this is all beside the point—or beside the cover-point, if you want to be comical, even though there aren't any more cover-points. What this article set out to do was to explain how hockey may be watched with a minimum of discomfort and an inside knowledge of the finer points of the game.

As it is necessary to have ice in order to play ice-hockey, I have invented a system, now in use in most rinks, whereby an artificial ice may be made by the passage of ammonia through pipes and one thing and

You can slip out and have a session with a frankfurter

another. The result is much the same as regular ice except that you can't use it in high-balls. It hurts just as much to fall down on and is just as easily fallen on as the real thing. In fact, it *is* ice, except that—well, as a matter of fact, although I invented the thing I can't explain it, and, what is more, I don't *want* to explain it. If you don't already know what artificial ice is, I don't care if you never know.

If you arrive at the hockey game just a little bit late, you will be able to annoy people around you by asking what has taken place since the game began. There is a place where the score is indicated, it is true, but it is difficult to find, especially if you come in late. In the Madison Square Garden in New York, where every night some different kind of sport is indulged in (one night, hockey; the next night, prize-fighting; the next night, bicycle-racing and so on and so forth) the same scoreboard is used except that the numbers are lighted up differently. I went to a hockey game late the other night and, looking up at the scoreboard, figured it out that Spandino and Milani had three more laps to go before they were three laps ahead of anyone else. This confused me a little, but not enough. I knew, in a way, that I was not at a bicycle race but I didn't feel in a position to argue with any scoreboard. So I went home rather than cause trouble.

Spectators at a hockey game, however, are generally pretty well up in the tactics of the game, always, as usual, excepting the women spectators. I would like to bet that a woman could have played hockey herself for five years and yet, if put among the spectators, wouldn't know what that man was doing with the little round disc.

55

However, poking fun at women for not knowing games is old stuff, and we must always remember that we men ourselves don't know everything about baking popovers. Not any more than women do. (Heh-heh!)

The man who thought of installing frankfurter stands in the lobbies of hockey arenas had a great idea. If it looks as if there might not be any scoring done for a long time (and, what with goal-tenders as efficient as they are, it most always does look that way) you can slip out and have a session with a frankfurter or even a bar of nougatine and get back in time to see the end of the period. The trouble with professional hockey as played today is that the goal-tenders are too good. A player may carry the puck down the ice as far as the goal and then, owing to the goal-tender's being just an old fool and not caring at all about the spectators, never get it in at all. This makes it difficult to get up any enthusiasm when you see things quickening up, because you know that nothing much will come of it anyway. My plan would be to eliminate the goal-tenders entirely and speed up the game. The officials could help some by sending them to the penalty box now and then.

As a matter of fact, I have never even seen a hockey game in my whole life.

A Good Old-Fashioned Christmas

SOONER or later at every Christmas party, just as things are beginning to get good, someone shuts his eyes, puts his head back and moans softly: "Ah, well, this isn't like the old days. We don't seem to have any good old-fashioned Christmases any more." To which the answer from my corner of the room is: "All right! That suits me!"

Just what they have in mind when they say "old-fashioned Christmas" you never can pin them down to telling. "Lots of snow," they mutter, "and lots of food." Yet, if you work it right, you can still get plenty of snow and food today. Snow, at any rate.

Then there seems to be some idea of the old-fashioned Christmas being, of necessity, in the country. It doesn't make any difference whether you were raised on a farm or whether your ideas of a rural Christmas were gleaned from pictures in old copies of "Harper's Young People," you must give folks to understand that such were the surroundings in which you spent your childhood holidays. And that, ah, me, those days will never come again!

Well, supposing you get your wish some time. Supposing, let us say, your wife's folks who live up in East Russet, Vermont, write and ask you to come up and bring the children for a good old-fashioned Christmas, "while we are all still together," they add cheerily with their flair for putting everybody in good humor.

Hurray, hurray! Off to the country for Christmas! Pack up all the warm clothes in the house, for you will need them up there where the air is clean and cold. Snow-shoes? Yes, put them in, or better yet, Daddy will carry them. What fun! Take along some sleigh-bells to jangle in case there aren't enough on the pung. There must be jangling sleigh-bells. And whisky for frost-bite. Or is it snake-bite that whisky is for? Anyway, put it in! We're off! Good-by, all! Good-by! JANGLE-JANGLE-JANGLE-Jangle-Jangle-Jangle-jangle-jangle-jangle-jangle-jangle-jangle!

In order to get to East Russet you take the Vermont Central as far as Twitchell's Falls and change there for Torpid River Junction, where a spur line takes you right into Gormley. At Gormley you are met by a buckboard which takes you back to Torpid River Junction again. By this time a train or something has come in which will wait for the local from Besus. While waiting for this you will have time to send your little boy to school, so that he can finish the third grade.

At East Russet Grandpa meets you with the sleigh. The bags are piled in and Mother sits in front with Lester in her lap while Daddy takes Junior and Ga-Ga in back with him and the luggage. Giddap, Esther Girl!

Esther Girl giddaps, and two suitcases fall out. Heigh-ho! Out we get and pick them up, brushing the snow off and filling our cuffs with it as we do so. After all, there is nothing like snow for getting up one's cuffs. Good clean snow never hurt anyone. Which is lucky, because after you have gone a mile or so, you discover that Ga-Ga is missing. Never mind, she is a self-reliant little girl and will doubtless find her way to the farm

58

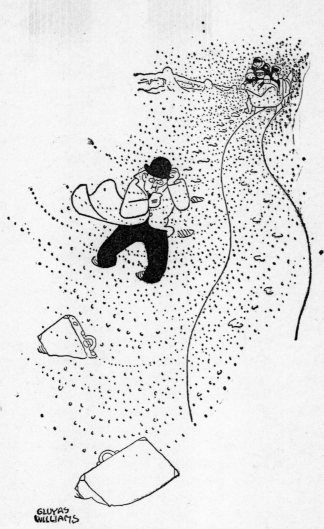

Esther Girl giddaps, and two suitcases fall out

by herself. Probably she will be there waiting for you when you arrive.

The farm is situated on a hill about eleven hundred miles from the center of town, just before you get into Canada. If there is a breeze in winter, they get it. But what do they care for breezes, so long as they have the Little Colonel oil-heater in the front room, to make everything cozy and warm within a radius of four inches! And the big open fireplace with the draught coming down it! Fun for everybody!

You are just driving up to the farmhouse in the sleigh, with the entire right leg frozen where the lap robe has slipped out. Grandma is waiting for you at the door and you bustle in, all glowing with good cheer. "Merry Christmas, Grandma!" Lester is cross and Junior is asleep and has to be dragged by the hand upstairs, bumping against each step all the way. It is so late that you decide that you all might as well go to bed, especially as you learn that breakfast is at four-thirty. It usually is at four, but Christmas being a holiday everyone sleeps late.

As you reach the top of the stairs you get into a current of cold air which has something of the quality of the temperature in a nice well-regulated crypt. This is the Bed Room Zone, and in it the thermometer never tops the zero mark from October fifteenth until the middle of May. Those rooms in which no one sleeps are used to store perishable vegetables in, and someone has to keep thumbing the tomatoes and pears every so often to prevent their getting so hard that they crack.

The way to get undressed for bed in one of Grandpa's bedrooms is as follows: Starting from the foot of the stairs where it is warm, run up two at a time to keep the circulation going as long as possible. Opening the bedroom door with one hand, tear down the curtains from the windows with the other, pick up the rugs from the floor and snatch the spread from the top of the bureau. Pile all these on the bed, cover with the closet door which you have wrenched from its hinges, and leap quickly underneath. It sometimes helps to put on a pair of rubbers over your shoes.

And even when you are in bed, you have no guarantee of going to sleep. Grandpa's mattresses seem to contain the overflow from the silo, corn-husks, baked-potato skins and long, stringy affairs which feel like pipe cleaners. On a cold night, snuggling down into these is about like snuggling down into a bed of damp pine cones out in the forest.

Then there are Things abroad in the house. Shortly after you get into bed, the stairs start snapping. Next something runs along the roof over your head. You say to yourself: "Don't be silly. It's only Santa Claus." Then it runs along in the wall behind the head of the bed. Santa Claus wouldn't do that. Down the long hall which leads into the ell of the house you can hear the wind sighing softly, with an occasional reassuring bang of a door.

The unmistakable sound of someone dying in great pain rises from just below the window-sill. It is a sort of low moan, with just a touch of strangulation in it. Perhaps Santa has fallen off the roof. Perhaps that story you once heard about Grandpa's house having been a hang-out for Revolutionary smugglers is true, and one of the smugglers has come back for his umbrella. The only place at a time like this is down under the bed-clothes. But the children become frightened and demand to be taken home, and Grandpa has to be called to explain that it is only Blue Bell out in the barn. Blue Bell has asthma, and on a cold night they have to be very patient with her.

Christmas morning dawns cloudy and cold, with the threat of plenty more snow, and, after all, what would Christmas be without snow? You lie in bed for one hour and a quarter trying to figure out how you can get up without losing the covers from around you. A glance at the water pitcher shows that it is time for them to put the red ball up for skating. You think of the nice warm bathroom at home, and decide that you can wait until you get back there before shaving.

This breaking the ice in the pitcher seems to be a feature of the early lives of all great men which they look back on with tremendous satisfaction. "When I was a boy, I used to have to break the ice in the pitcher every morning before I could wash," is said with as much pride as one might say, "When I was a boy I stood at the head of my class." Just what virtue there is in having to break ice in a pitcher is not evident, unless it lies in their taking the bother to break the ice and wash at all. Anytime that I have to break ice in a pitcher as a preliminary to washing, I go unwashed, that's all. And Benjamin Franklin and U. S. Grant and Rutherford B. Hayes can laugh as much as they like. I'm nobody's fool about a thing like that.

Getting the children dressed is a lot of fun when you have to keep pumping their limbs up and down to keep them from freezing out stiff. The children love it and

63

are just as bright and merry as little pixies when it is time to go downstairs and say "Good morning" to Grandpa and Grandma. The entire family enters the dining-room purple and chattering and exceedingly cross.

The entire family enters, purple and chattering and exceedingly cross

After breakfast everyone begins getting dinner. The kitchen being the only warm place in the house may have something to do with it. But before long there are so many potato peelings and turkey feathers and squash seeds and floating bits of pie crust in the kitchen that the women-folk send you and the children off into the

64

front part of the house to amuse yourselves and get out of the way.

Then what a jolly time you and the kiddies and Grandpa have together! You can either slide on the horse-hair sofa, or play "The Wayside Chapel" on the piano (the piano has scroll-work on either side of the music rack with yellow silk showing through), or look out the window and see ten miles of dark gray snow. Perhaps you may even go out to the barn and look at the horses and cows, but really, as you walk down between the stalls, when you have seen one horse or one cow you have seen them all. And besides, the cold in the barn has an added flavor of damp harness leather and musty carriage upholstery which eats into your very marrow.

Of course, there are the presents to be distributed, but that takes on much the same aspect as the same ceremony in the new-fashioned Christmas, except that in the really old-fashioned Christmas the presents weren't so tricky. Children got mostly mittens and shoes, with a sled thrown in sometimes for dissipation. Where a boy today is bored by three o'clock in the afternoon with his electric grain-elevator and miniature pond with real perch in it, the old-fashioned boy was lucky if he got a copy of "Naval Battles of the War of 1812" and an orange. Now this feature is often brought up in praise of the old way of doing things. "I tell you," says Uncle Gyp, "the children in my time never got such presents as you get today." And he seems proud of the fact, as if there were some virtue accruing to him for it. If the children of today can get electric grain-elevators and tin automobiles for Christmas, why aren't they that much better off than

65

their grandfathers who got only wristlets? Learning the value of money, which seems to be the only argument of the stand-patters, doesn't hold very much water as a Christmas slogan. The value of money can be learned in just about five minutes when the time comes, but Christmas is not the season.

But to return to the farm, where you and the kiddies and Gramp' are killing time. You can either bring in wood from the woodshed, or thaw out the pump, or read the books in the bookcase over the writing-desk. Of the three, bringing in the wood will probably be the most fun, as you are likely to burn yourself thawing out the pump, and the list of reading matter on hand includes "The Life and Deeds of General Grant," "Our First Century," "Andy's Trip to Portland," bound volumes of the Jersey Cattle Breeders' Gazette and "Diseases of the Horse." Then there are some old copies of "Round the Lamp" for the years 1850-54 and some colored plates showing plans for the approaching World's Fair at Chicago.

Thus the time passes, in one round of gayety after another, until you are summoned to dinner. Here all caviling must cease. The dinner lives up to the advertising. If an old-fashioned Christmas could consist entirely of dinner without the old-fashioned bedrooms, the old-fashioned pitcher, and the old-fashioned entertainments, we professional pessimists wouldn't have a turkey-leg left to stand on. But, as has been pointed out, it is possible to get a good dinner without going up to East Russet, Vt., or, if it isn't, then our civilization has been a failure.

And the dinner only makes the aftermath seem worse.

66

According to an old custom of the human race, everyone overeats. Deliberately and with considerable gusto you sit at the table and say pleasantly: "My, but I won't be able to walk after this. Just a little more of the dark

Then you sit and moan

meat, please, Grandpa, and just a dab of stuffing. Oh, dear, that's too much!" You haven't the excuse of the drunkard, who becomes oblivious to his excesses after several drinks. You know what you are doing, and yet you make light of it and even laugh about it as long as you *can* laugh without splitting out a seam.

And then you sit and moan. If you were having a good new-fashioned Christmas you could go out to the movies or take a walk, or a ride, but to be really old-fashioned you must stick close to the house, for in the old days there were no movies and no automobiles and if you wanted to take a walk you had to have the hired man go ahead of you with a snow-shovel and make a tunnel. There are probably plenty of things to do in the country today, and just as many automobiles and electric lights as there are in the city, but you can't call Christmas with all these improvements "an old-fashioned Christmas." That's cheating.

If you are going through with the thing right, you have got to retire to the sitting-room after dinner and *sit*. Of course, you can go out and play in the snow if you want to, but you know as well as I do that this playing in the snow is all right when you are small but a bit trying on anyone over thirty. And anyway, it always began to snow along about three in the afternoon an old-fashioned Christmas day, with a cheery old leaden sky overhead and a jolly old gale sweeping around the corners of the house.

No, you simply must sit indoors, in front of a fire if you insist, but nevertheless with nothing much to do. The children are sleepy and snarling. Grandpa is just sleepy. Someone tries to start the conversation, but everyone else is too gorged with food to be able to move the lower jaw sufficiently to articulate. It develops that the family is in possession of the loudest-ticking clock in the world and along about four o'clock it begins to break its own record. A stenographic report of the proceedings would read as follows:

"Ho-hum! I'm sleepy! I shouldn't have eaten so much."

"Tick-tock-tick-tock-tick-tock-tick-tock—"

"It seems just like Sunday, doesn't it?"

"Look at Grandpa! He's asleep."

"Here, Junior! Don't plague Grandpa. Let him sleep."

"Tick-tock-tick-tock-tick-tock—"

"Junior! Let Grandpa alone! Do you want Mamma to take you up-stairs?"

"Ho-hum!"

"Tick-tock-tick-tock-tick-tock—"

Louder and louder the clock ticks, until something snaps in your brain and you give a sudden leap into the air with a scream, finally descending to strangle each of the family in turn, and Grandpa as he sleeps. Then, as you feel your end is near, all the warm things you have ever known come back to you, in a flash. You remember the hot Sunday subway to Coney, your trip to Mexico, the bull-fighters of Spain.

You dash out into the snowdrifts and plunge along until you sink exhausted. Only the fact that this article ends here keeps you from freezing to death, with an obituary the next day reading:

"DIED suddenly, at East Russet, Vt., of an old-fashioned Christmas."

The New Wing

(Or That Sagredo Bed)

ALTHOUGH the new wing of the Metropolitan Museum of Art ("Wing K," if that makes it any easier for you) was opened some time ago, I have only just this week got around to inspecting it. I'm sorry.

"Wing K" has, since 1916, been empty, and, although passers-by late at night have often reported strange noises coming from its vast recesses, the Museum officials stubbornly maintain that it has been put to absolutely no use at all. This sounds a little fishy to me, however, and if those old walls could talk we might learn a little something more about where Mr. Munsey's money went. It is said that only a couple of hundred dollars remain of all the millions that he bequeathed to the Museum. Money doesn't *fly* away, you know.

At any rate, "Wing K" is full now and it takes a good twenty minutes of fast walking to see everything in it. This does not include the time taken up in getting lost or in walking through the same hall twice.

My inspection was somewhat hampered by having Mr. Charles MacGreggor along with me. Mr. MacGreggor kept constantly asking to see Dr. Crippen. "I want to see Dr. Crippen," he would say, or "Where is Dr. Crippen?" I told him that the wax-works were in another wing of the Museum, but someone had told him that a replica of Dr. Crippen was to be found in "Wing K" and nothing would do but he must see it. Along toward the end, as

As Mr. MacGreggor got tired and cross he began sniveling

Mr. MacGreggor got tired and cross, he began sniveling and crying, "I want to see Dr. Crippen" so loudly that an attendant put us out. So we probably missed some of the funniest parts of the exhibit. If you want me to I will go up again sometime without Mr. MacGreggor. Or maybe Dr. Crippen *is* there, after all.

The feature of the new wing is, of course, the Bedroom from the Palazzo Sagredo at Venice. The best way that I can describe it is to say that it is fully twice the size of our guest room in Scarsdale, and fifty per cent fancier. The chief point in favor of our guest room in Scarsdale is that there isn't a whole troop of people strolling through it at all hours of the day, peeking under the bed and asking questions about it. If you want to sleep after nine in the morning in Scarsdale you can do it without being made an exhibition of. My two little boys may romp into the room three or four times during the morning to show you an engine or a snake, but all that you have to do is to tell them to get the hell out or you will tell me on them.

The owner of the Palazzo Sagredo was a great cupid fancier. Over the doorway to the alcove where the bed is, there are over a dozen great, big cupids stuck on the wall, like mosquitoes in a summer hotel. They are heavy, hulking things and seem to have fulfilled no good purpose except possibly to confuse any guest who may have retired to the fancy bed with a snootful of good red Sagredo wine. To awaken from the first heavy sleep of a Venetian bun and see fifteen life-sized cupids dangling from the doorway must have been an experience to send the eighteenth-century guest into a set of early eighteenth-century or late seventeenth-century heebies. The comic strip on the ceiling is catalogued as "Diziani's Dawn." It may very well be.

This, in a general way, covers pretty well the Bedroom from the Palazzo Sagredo. In another month the Gideons will have slipped a Bible onto the table by the bed and it will be ready for occupancy, but not by *me*, thank you.

Walking rapidly through the rest of the new wing, you come to lots of things in cases which, frankly, do *not* look very interesting. There is a bit of sculpture labeled "Head of Zeus (?)" showing that even the Museum officials don't know whom it is meant to represent. Under the circumstances, it seems as if they might have cheated a little and thrown a bluff by just calling it arbitrarily "Head of Zeus" without the question mark. Certainly no one could have called them on it, and it would have made them seem a little less afraid to take a chance. Suppose that it turned out *not* to be Zeus. What is the worst that could happen to them?

Then, too, there is "A Relief from a Roman Sarcophagus." As we remember Roman sarcophagi, *anything* would be a relief from them.

We could go on like this for page after page making wise-cracks about the various uninteresting features of the new wing, but perhaps you have already got the idea. It may have been the absence of Dr. Crippen, or it may have been a new pair of shoes, but the truth is that we weren't *put* out of the new wing. We *asked* an attendant how to *get* out. And here we are.

When Genius Remained Your Humble Servant

O F COURSE, I really know nothing about it, but I would be willing to wager that the last words of Penelope, as Odysseus bounced down the front steps, bag in hand, were: "Now, don't forget to write, Odie. You'll find some papyrus rolled up in your clean peplum, and just drop me a line on it whenever you get a chance."

And ever since that time people have been promising to write, and then explaining why they haven't written. Most personal correspondence of to-day consists of letters the first half of which are given over to an indexed statement of reasons why the writer hasn't written before, followed by one paragraph of small talk, with the remainder devoted to reasons why it is imperative that the letter be brought to a close. So many people begin their letters by saying that they have been rushed to death during the last month, and therefore haven't found time to write, that one wonders where all the grown persons come from who attend movies at eleven in the morning. There has been a misunderstanding of the word "busy" somewhere.

So explanatory has the method of letter writing become that it is probable that if Odysseus were a modern traveler his letters home to Penelope would average something like this:

Calypso,
Friday afternoon.

DEAR PEN:—I have been so tied up with work during the last week that I haven't had a chance to get near a desk to write to you. I have been trying to every day, but something would come up just at the last minute that would prevent me. Last Monday I got the papyrus all unrolled, and then I had to tend to Scylla and Charybdis (I may have written you about them before), and by the time I got through with them it was bedtime, and, believe me, I am snatching every bit of sleep I can get these days. And so it went, first the Læstrygones, and then something else, and here it is Friday. Well, there isn't much news to write about. Things are going along here about as usual. There is a young nymph here who seems to own the place, but I haven't had any chance to meet her socially. Well, there goes the ship's bell. I guess I had better be bringing this to a close. I have got a lot of work to do before I get dressed to go to a dinner of that nymph I was telling you about. I have met her brother, and he and I are interested in the same line of goods. He was at Troy with me. Well, I guess I must be closing. Will try to get off a longer letter in a day or two.

Your loving husband,

ODIE.

P.S.—You haven't got that bunch of sports hanging round the palace still, have you? Tell Telemachus I'll take him out of school if I hear of his playing around with any of them.

But there was a time when letter writing was such a fad, especially among the young girls, that if they had

76

had to choose between eating three meals a day and writing a letter they wouldn't have given the meals even a consideration. In fact, they couldn't do both, for the length of maidenly letters in those days precluded any time out for meals. They may have knocked off for a few minutes during the heat of the day for a whiff at a bottle of salts, but to nibble at anything heartier than lettuce would have cramped their style.

Take Miss Clarissa Harlowe, for instance. In Richardson's book (which, in spite of my personal aversion to it, has been hailed by every great writer, from Pope to Stevenson, as being perfectly bully) she is given the opportunity of telling 2,400 closely printed pages full of story by means of letters to her female friend, Miss Howe (who plays a part similar to the orchestra leader in Frank Tinney's act). And 2,400 pages is nothing to her. When the book closes she is just beginning to get her stride. As soon as she got through with that she probably sat down and wrote a series of letters to the London papers about the need for conscription to fight the Indians in America.

To a girl like Clarissa, in the middle of the eighteenth century, no day was too full of horrors, no hour was too crowded with terrific happenings to prevent her from seating herself at a desk (she must have carried the desk about with her, strapped over her shoulder) and tearing off twenty or thirty pages to Friend Anna, telling her all about it. The only way that I can see in which she could accomplish this so efficiently would be to have a copy boy standing at her elbow, who took the letter, sheet by sheet, as she wrote it, and dashed with it to the printer.

It is hard to tell just which a girl of that period considered more important, the experiences she was writing of or the letter itself. She certainly never slighted the letter. If the experience wanted to overtake her, and jump up on the desk beside her, all right, but, experience or no experience, she was going to get that letter in the next post or die in the attempt. Unfortunately, she never died in the attempt.

Thus, an attack on a young lady's house by a band of cutthroats, resulting in the burning of the structure and her abduction, might have been told of in the eighteenth century letter system as follows:

Monday night.

SWEET ANNA:—At this writing I find myself in the most horrible circumstance imaginable. Picture to yourself, if you can, my dear Anna, a party of villainous brigands, veritable cutthroats, all of them, led by a surly fellow in green alpaca with white insertion, breaking their way, by very force, through the side of your domicile, like so many ugly intruders, and threatening you with vile imprecations to make you disclose the hiding place of the family jewels. If the mere thought of such a contingency is painful to you, my beloved Anna, consider what it means to me, your delicate friend, to whom it is actually happening at this very minute! For such is in very truth the situation which is disclosing itself in my room as I write. Not three feet away from me is the odious person before described. Now he is threatening me with renewed vigor! Now he has placed his coarse hands on my throat, completely hiding the pearl necklace which papa brought me from Epsom last summer, and which you, and also young Pindleson (whose very name I mention with a blush), have so often admired. But more of this later, and until then, believe me, my dear Anna, to be

Your ever distressed and affectionate

CL. HARLOWE.

Monday night. Later.

DEAREST ANNA:—Now, indeed, it is evident, my best, my old friend, that I am face to face with the bitterest of fates. You will remember that in my last letter I spoke to you of a party of unprincipled knaves who were invading my apartment. And now do I find that they have, in furtherance of their inexcusable plans, set fire to that portion of the house which lies directly behind this, so that as I put my pen to paper the flames are creeping, like hungry creatures of some sort, through the partitions and into this very room, so that did I esteem my safety more than my correspondence with you, my precious companion, I should at once be making preparation for immediate departure. O my dear! To be thus seized, as I am at this very instant, by the unscrupulous leader of the band and carried, by brute force, down the stairway through the butler's pantry and into the servants' hall, writing as I go, resting my poor paper cn the shoulder of my detested abductor, is truly, you will agree, my sweet Anna, a pitiable episode.

Adieu, my intimate friend.

Your obt. s'v't,

CL. HARLOWE.

79

One, wonders (or, at least, *I* wonder, and that is sufficient for the purposes of this article) what the letter-writing young lady of that period would have done had she lived in this day of postcards showing the rocks at Scipawisset or the Free Public Library in East Tarvia. She might have used them for some of her shorter messages, but I rather doubt it. The foregoing scene could hardly have been done justice to on a card bearing the picture of the Main Street of the town, looking north from the Soldiers' Monument, with the following legend:

"Our house is the third on the left with the lilac bush. Cross marks window where gang of roughnecks have just broken in and are robbing and burning the house. Looks like a bad night. Wish you were here.   C. H."

No; that would never have done, but it would have been a big relief for the postilion, or whoever it was that had to carry Miss Clarissa's effusions to their destination. The mail on Monday morning, after a spring-like Sunday, must have been something in the nature of a wagon load of rolls of news print that used to be seen standing in front of newspaper offices in the good old days when newspapers were printed on paper stock. Of course, the postilion had the opportunity of whiling away the time between stations by reading some of the spicier bits in the assortment, but even a postilion must have had his feelings, and a man can't read that kind of stuff *all* of the time, and still keep his health.

Of course, there are a great many people now who write letters because they like to. Also, there are some who do it because they feel that they owe it to posterity

"To be thus seized . . . is truly, you will agree, my sweet Anna, a pitiable episode"

and to their publishers to do so. As soon as a man begins to sniff a chance that he may become moderately famous he is apt to brush up on his letter writing and never send anything out that has not been polished and proofread, with the idea in mind that some day some one is going to get all of his letter together and make a book of them. Apparently, most great men whose letters have been published have had premonition of their greatness when quite young, as their childish letters bear the marks of careful and studied attention to publicity values. One can almost imagine the budding genius, aged eight, sitting at his desk and saying to himself:

"I must not forget that I am now going through the 'Sturm und Drang' period"

"In this spontaneous letter to my father I must not forget that I am now going through the *Sturm und Drang* (storm and stress) period of my youth and that this letter will have to be grouped by the compiler

83

under the *Sturm und Drang* (storm and stress) section
in my collected letters. I must therefore keep in the key
and quote only such of my favorite authors as will contribute to the effect. I think I will use Werther today.
. . . My dear Father"—etc.

I have not known many geniuses in their youth, but
I have had several youths pointed out to me by their
parents as geniuses, and I must confess that I have
never seen a letter from any one of them that differed
greatly from the letters of a normal boy, unless perhaps
they were spelled less accurately. Given certain uninteresting conditions, let us say, at boarding school, and
I believe that the average bright boy's letter home would
read something in this fashion:

> Exeter, N. H.,
> Wed., April 25.

MY DEAR FATHER AND MOTHER:

I have been working pretty hard this week, studying
for a history examination, and so haven't had much of
a chance to write to you. Everything is about the same
as usual here, and there doesn't seem to be much news
to write to you about. The box came all right, and thank
you very much. All the fellows liked it, especially the
little apple pies. Thank you very much for sending it.
There hasn't much been happening here since I wrote
you last week. I had to buy a new pair of running
drawers, which cost me fifty cents. Does that come out
of my allowance? Or will you pay for it? There doesn't
seem to be any other news. Well, there goes the bell, so
I guess I will be closing.

> Your loving son,
> BUXTON.

84

Given the same, even less interesting conditions, and a boy such as Stevenson must have been (judging from his letters) could probably have delivered himself of this, and more, too:

> *Wyckham-Wyckham,*
> *The Tenth.*

DEAR PATER:—To-day has been unbelievably exquisite! Great, undulating clouds, rolling in serried formation across a sky of pure *lapis lazuli.* I feel like what Updike calls a "myrmidon of unhesitating amplitude." And a perfect gem of a letter from Toto completed the felicitous experience. You would hardly believe, and yet you must, in your *cœur des cœurs,* know, that the brown, esoteric hills of this Oriental retreat affect me like the red wine of Russilon, and, indigent as I am in these matters, I cannot but feel that you have, as Herbert says:

> *"Carve or discourse; do not a famine fear.*
> *Who carves is kind to two, who talks to all."*

Yesterday I saw a little native boy, a veritable boy of the streets, playing at a game at once so naïve and so resplendent that I was irresistibly drawn to its contemplation. You will doubtless jeer when I tell you. He was tossing a small *blatch,* such as grow in great profusion here, to and fro between himself and the wall of the *limple.* I was stunned for the moment, and then I realized that I was looking into the very soul of the peasantry, the open stigma of the nation. How queer it all seemed! Did it not?

You doubtless think me an ungrateful fellow for

not mentioning the delicious assortment of goodies which came, like melons to Artemis, to this benighted *gesellschaft* on Thursday last. They were devoured to the last crumb, and I was reminded as we ate, like so many *wurras*, of those lines of that gorgeous Herbert, of whom I am so fond:

> *"Must all be veiled, while he that reads divines,*
> *Catching the sense at two removes?"*

The breeze is springing up, and it brings to me messages of the open meadows of Litzel, deep festooned with the riot of gloriannas. How quiet they seem to me as I think of them now! How emblematic! Do you know, my dear Parent, that I sometimes wonder if, after all, it were not better to dream, and dream . . . and dream.

Your affectionate son,

BERGQUIST.

So don't worry about your boy if he writes home like that. He may simply have an eye for fame and future compilation.

Shakespeare Explained

Carrying on the System of Footnotes to a Silly Extreme

PERICLES

ACT II. SCENE 3

Enter first Lady-in-Waiting (Flourish,[1] Hautboys[2] and[3] torches[4]).

First Lady-in-Waiting—What[5] ho![6] Where[7] is[8] the[9] music?[10]

NOTES

1. *Flourish:* The stage direction here is obscure. Clarke claims it should read "flarish," thus changing the meaning of the passage to "flarish" (that is, the King's), but most authorities have agreed that it should remain "flourish," supplying the predicate which is to be flourished. There was at this time a custom in the countryside of England to flourish a mop as a signal to the passing vender of berries, signifying that in that particular household there was a consumer-demand for berries, and this may have been meant in this instance. That Shakespeare was cognizant of this custom of flourishing the mop for berries is shown in a similar passage in the second part of King Henry IV, where he has the Third Page enter and say, "Flourish." Cf. also Hamlet, IV, 7: 4.

2. *Hautboys,* from the French *haut,* meaning "high" and the Eng. *boys,* meaning "boys." The

word here is doubtless used in the sense of "high boys," indicating either that Shakespeare intended to convey the idea of spiritual distress on the part of the First Lady-in-Waiting or that he did not. Of this Rolfe says: "Here we have one of the chief indications of Shakespeare's knowledge of human na-

"Might be one of the hautboys bearing a box of 'trognies' for the actors to suck"

ture, his remarkable insight into the petty foibles of this work-a-day world." Cf. T. N. 4: 6, "Mine eye hath play'd the painter, and hath stell'd thy beauty's form in table of my heart."

3. *and.* A favorite conjunctive of Shakespeare's in referring to the need for a more adequate navy for England. Tauchnitz claims that it should be pronounced

"und," stressing the anti-penult. This interpretation, however, has found disfavor among most commentators because of its limited significance. We find the same conjunctive in A. W. T. E. W. 6: 7, "Steel-boned, unyielding *and* uncomplying virtue," and here there can be no doubt that Shakespeare meant that if the King should consent to the marriage of his daughter the excuse of Stephano, offered in Act 2, would carry no weight.

4. *Torches.* The interpolation of some foolish player and never the work of Shakespeare (Warb.). The critics of the last century have disputed whether or not this has been misspelled in the original, and should read "trochies" or "troches." This might well be since the introduction of tobacco into England at this time had wrought havoc with the speaking voices of the players, and we might well imagine that at the entrance of the First Lady-in-Waiting there might be perhaps one of the hautboys mentioned in the preceding passage bearing a box of troches or "trognies" for the actors to suck. Of this entrance Clarke remarks: "The noble mixture of spirited firmness and womanly modesty, fine sense and true humility, clear sagacity and absence of conceit, passionate warmth and sensitive delicacy, generous love and self-diffidence with which Shakespeare has endowed this First Lady-in-Waiting renders her in our eyes one of the most admirable of his female characters." Cf. M. S. N. D. 8: 9, "That solder'st close impossibilities and mak'st them kiss."

5. *What*—What.

6. *Ho!* In conjunction with the preceding word doubtless means "What ho!" changed by Clarke to

"What hoo!" In the original MS. it reads "What hi!" but this has been accredited to the tendency of the time to write "What hi" when "what ho" was meant. Techner alone maintains that it should read "What humpf!" Cf. Ham. 5: o, "High-ho!"

7. *Where.* The reading of the folio, retained by Johnson, the Cambridge editors and others, but it is not impossible that Shakespeare wrote "why," as Pope and others give it. This would make the passage read "Why the music?" instead of "Where is the music?" and would be a much more probable interpretation in view of the music of that time. Cf. George Ade. Fable No. 15, "Why the gunnysack?"

8. *is*—is not. That is, would not be.

9. *the.* Cf. Ham. 4: 6. M. S. N. D. 3: 5. A. W. T. E. W. 2: 6. T. N. 1: 3 and Macbeth 3: 1, "that knits up *the* raveled sleeves of care."

10. *music.* Explained by Malone as "the art of making music" or "music that is made." If it has but one of these meanings we are inclined to think it is the first; and this seems to be favored by what precedes, "*the* music!" Cf. M. of V. 4: 2, "The man that hath no music in himself."

The meaning of the whole passage seems to be that the First Lady-in-Waiting has entered concomitant with a flourish, hautboys and torches and says, "What ho! Where is the music?"

Gardening Notes

DURING the past month almost every paper, with the exception of the agricultural journals, has installed an agricultural department, containing short articles by the proprietor or some one else in the office who had an unoccupied typewriter, telling the American citizen how to start and hold the interest of a small garden. The seed catalogue has become the catechism of the patriot, and, if you don't like to read the brusk, prosy directions on planting as given there, you may find the same thing done in verse in your favorite poetry magazine, or a special department in *The Plumbing Age* under the heading "The Plumber's Garden: How and When to Plant."

But all of these editorial suggestions appear to be conducted by professionals for the benefit of the layman, which seems to me to be a rather one-sided way of going about the thing. Obviously the suggestions should come from a layman himself, in the nature of warnings to others.

I am qualified to put forth such an article because of two weeks' service in my own back-yard, doing my bit for Peter Henderson and planting all sorts of things in the ground without the slightest expectation of ever seeing anything of any of them again. If, by any chance, a sprout should show itself, unmistakably the result of one of my plantings, I would be willing to be quoted as saying that Nature *is* wonderful. In fact, I would take it as a personal favor, and would feel that anything that I might do in the future for Nature would be little enough in return for the special work she went to all the trouble of doing for me. But all of this is on condition that something of mine grows into manhood. Otherwise, Nature can go her way and I'll go mine, just as we have gone up till now.

However, although I am an amateur, I shall have to adopt, in my writing, the tone of a professional, or I shall never get any one to believe what I say. If, therefore, from now on I sound a bit cold and unfriendly, you will realize that a professional agricultural writer has to have *some* dignity about his stuff, and that beneath my rough exterior I am a pleasant enough sort of person to meet socially.

Preparing the Ground for the Garden

This is one of the most important things that the young gardener is called upon to do. In fact, a great many young gardeners never do anything further. Some inherited weakness, something they never realized they had before, may crop out during this process: weak back, tendency of shoulder blades to ossification, misplacement of several important vertebrae, all are apt to be discovered for the first time during the course of one day's digging. If, on the morning following the first attempt to prepare the ground for planting, you are able to walk in a semi-erect position as far as the bath-tub (and, without outside assistance, lift one foot into the water), you may flatter yourself that you are, joint for joint, in as perfect condition as the man in the rubber-heels advertisements.

Authorities differ as to the best way of digging. All agree that it is impossible to avoid walking about during the following week as if you were impersonating an old colored waiter with the lumbago; but there are two schools, each with its own theory, as to the less painful

"If you are able to walk as far as the bathtub . . ."

method. One advocates bending over, without once raising up, until the whole row is dug. The others, of whom I must confess that I am one, feel that it is better to draw the body to a more-or-less erect position after each shovelful. In support of this contention, Greitz, the well-known authority on the muscles of the back, says on page 233 of his "Untersuchungen über Sittlichkeitsdelikte und Gesellschaftsbiologie":

"The constant tightening and relaxing of the

93

latissimus dorsi effected in raising the body as the earth is tossed aside, has a tendency to relieve the strain by distributing it equally among the *serratus posticus inferior* and the corner of Thirty-fourth Street." He then goes on to say practically what I have said above.

The necessity for work of such a strenuous nature in the mere preliminaries of the process of planting a garden is due to the fact that the average back-yard has, up till the present time, been behaving less like a garden than anything else in the world. You might think that a back-yard, possessed of an ordinary amount of decency and civic-pride would, at some time during its career, have said to itself:

"Now look here! I may some day be called upon to be a garden, and the least I can do is to get myself into some sort of shape, so that, when the time comes, I will be fairly ready to receive a seed or two."

But no! Year in and year out they have been drifting along in a fools' paradise, accumulating stones and queer, indistinguishable cans and things, until they were prepared to become anything, quarries, iron-mines, notion-counters—anything but gardens.

I have saved in a box all the things that I have dug from my back-yard, and, when I have them assembled, all I will need will be a good engine to make them into a pretty fairly decent runabout—nothing elaborate, mind you, but good enough to run the family out in on Sunday afternoons.

And then there are lots of other things that wouldn't even fit into the runabout. Queer-looking objects, they are; things that perhaps in their heyday were rather stunning, but which have now assumed an air of indifference, as if to say, "Oh, call me anything, old fellow, Ice-pick, Mainspring, Cigar-lighter, anything, I don't care." I tell you, it's enough to make a man stop and think. But there, I mustn't get sentimental.

In preparing the soil for planting, you will need several tools. Dynamite would be a beautiful thing to use, but it would have a tendency to get the dirt into the front-hall and track up the stairs. This not being practicable, there is no other way but for you to get at it with a fork (oh, don't be silly), a spade, and a rake. If you have an empty and detached furnace boiler, you might bring that along to fill with the stones you will dig up. If it is a small garden, you ought not to have to empty the boiler more than three or four times. Any neighbor who is building a stone house will be glad to contract with you for the stones, and those that are left over after he has got his house built can be sold to another neighbor who is building another stone house. Your market is limited only by the number of neighbors who are building stone houses.

On the first day, when you find yourself confronted by a stretch of untouched ground which is to be turned over (technical phrase, meaning to "turn over"), you may be somewhat at a loss to know where to begin. Such indecision is only natural, and should cause no worry on the part of the young gardener. It is something we all have to go through with. You may feel that it would be futile and unsystematic to go about digging up a forkful here and a shovelful there, tossing the earth at random, in the hope that in due time you will get the place dug up. And so it would.

The thing to do is to decide just where you want your

95

garden, and what its dimensions are to be. This will have necessitated a previous drawing up of a chart, showing just what is to be planted and where. As this chart will be the cause of considerable hard feeling in the family circle, usually precipitating a fist-fight over the number of rows of onions to be set out, I will not touch on that in this article. There are some things too intimate for even a professional agriculturist to write of. I will say, however, that those in the family who are

"Make a rather impressive ceremony of driving the first stake"

standing out for onions might much better save their time and feelings by pretending to give in, and then, later in the day, sneaking out and slipping the sprouts in by themselves in some spot where they will know where to find them again.

Having decided on the general plan and dimensions of the plot, gather the family about as if for a cornerstone dedication, and then make a rather impressive ceremony of driving in the first stake by getting your little boy to sing the first twelve words of some patriotic air. (If he doesn't know the first twelve, any twelve will do. The idea is to keep the music going during the driving of the stake.)

The stake is to be driven at an imaginary corner of what is to be your garden, and a string stretched to another stake at another imaginary corner, and there you have a line along which to dig. This will be a big comfort. You will feel that at last you have something tangible. Now all that remains is to turn the ground over, harrow it, smooth it up nice and neat, plant your seeds, cultivate them, thin out your plants and pick the crops.

It may seem that I have spent most of my time in advice on preparing the ground for planting. Such may well be the case, as that was as far as I got. I then found a man who likes to do those things and whose doctor has told him that he ought to be out of doors all the time. He is an Italian, and charges really very little when you consider what he accomplishes. Any further advice on starting and keeping up a garden, I shall have to get him to write for you.

The Passing of the Orthodox Paradox

WHATEVER irreparable harm may have been done to Society by the recent epidemic of crook, sex and other dialect plays, one great alleviation has resulted. They have driven up-stage, for the time being, the characters who exist on tea and repartee in "The drawing-room of Sir Arthur Peaversham's town house, Grosvenor Square. Time: late Autumn."

A person in a crook play may have talked underworld patois which no self-respecting criminal would have allowed himself to utter, but he did not sit on a divan and evolve abnormal *bons mots* with each and every breath. The misguided and misinformed daughter in the Self and Sex Play may have lisped words which only an interne should hear, but she did not offer a succession of brilliant but meaningless paradoxes as a substitute for real conversation.

Continuously snappy back-talk is now encountered chiefly in such acts as those of "Cooney & LeBlanc, the Eccentric Comedy Dancing Team." And even *they* manage to scrape along without the paradoxes.

But there was a time, beginning with the Oscar Wilde era, when no unprotected thought was safe. It might be seized at any moment by an English Duke or a Lady Agatha and strangled to death. Even the butlers in the late 'eighties were wits, and served epigrams with cucumber sandwiches; and a person entering one of these drawing-rooms and talking in connected sentences —easily understood by everybody—each with one subject, predicate and meaning, would have been looked

"Snappy back-talk is now encountered chiefly in such acts as 'Cooney and Le Blanc, the Eccentric Comedy Dancing Team'"

upon as a high-class moron. One might as well have gone to a dinner at Lady Coventry's without one's collar, as without one's kit of trained paradoxes.

A late Autumn afternoon in one of these semi-Oscar Wilde plays, for instance, would run something like this:

SCENE—*The Octagon Room in Lord Raymond Eaveston's Manor House in Stropshire.*

LADY EAVESTON *and* SIR THOMAS WAFFLETON *are discovered, arranging red flowers in a vase.*

SIR T.: I detest red flowers; they are so yellow.

LADY E.: What a cynic you are, Sir Thomas. I really must not listen to you or I shall hear something that you say.

99

SIR T.: Not at all, my dear Lady Eaveston. I detest people who listen closely; they are so inattentive.

LADY E.: Pray do not be analytical, my dear Sir Thomas. When people are extremely analytical with me I am sure that they are superficial, and, to me, nothing is more abominable than superficiality, unless perhaps it is an intolerable degree of thoroughness.

"The butlers served epigrams with the cucumber sandwiches"

(Enter Meadows, the Butler)

MEADOWS *(announcing)*: Sir Mortimer Longley and Mrs. Wrennington—a most remarkable couple—I may say in announcing them—in that there is nothing at all remarkable about them.

(Enter Sir Mortimer and Mrs. Wrennington)

MRS. W.: So sorry to be late, dear Lady Eaveston. But it is so easy to be on time that I always make it a point to be late. It lends poise, and poise is a charming quality for any woman to have, am I not right, Sir Thomas?

Sir T.: You are always right, my dear Mrs. Wrennington, and never more so than now, for I know of no more attractive attribute than poise, unless perhaps it be embarrassment.

Lady E.: What horrid cynics you men are! Really, Sir Thomas, one might think, from your sophisticated remarks that you had been brought up in the country and had seen nothing of life.

Sir T.: And so I *have* been, my dear Lady Eaveston. To my mind, London is nothing but the country, and certainly Stropshire is nothing but a metropolis. The difference is, that when one is in town, one lives with others, and when one is in the country, others live with one. And both plans are abominable.

Mrs. W.: What a horrid combination! I hate horrid combinations; they always turn out to be so extremely pleasant.

(Enter Meadows)

Meadows *(announcing)*: Sir Roland Pinshamton; Viscount Lemingham; Countess Trotski and Mr. Peters. In announcing these parties I cannot refrain from remarking that it has always been my opinion that a man who intends to get married should either know something or nothing, preferably both.

(Exit Meadows)

Countess T.: So sorry to be late, my dear Lady Eaveston. It was charmingly tolerant of you to have us.

Lady E.: Invitations are never tolerant, my dear Countess; acceptances always are. But do tell me, how is your husband, the Count—or perhaps he is no longer your husband. One never knows these days whether a

101

man is his wife's husband or whether she is simply his wife.

COUNTESS T. (*lighting a cigarette*) : Really, Lady Eaveston, you grow more and more interesting. I detest interesting people; they are so hopelessly uninteresting. It is like beautiful people—who are usually so singularly unbeautiful. Has not that been your experience, Sir Mortimer?

SIR M.: May I have the pleasure of escorting you to the music-room, Mrs. Wrennington?

(*Exeunt omnes to music-room for dinner*)
Curtain.

It is from this that we have, in a measure, been delivered by the court-room scenes, and all the medical dramas. But the paradox still remains intrenched in English writing behind Mr. G. K. Chesterton, and he may be considered, by literary tacticians, as considerable stronghold.

Here again we find our commonplaces shaken up until they emerge in what looks like a new and tremendously imposing shape, and all of them ostensibly proving the opposite of what we have always understood. If we do not quite catch the precise meaning at first reading, we lay it to our imperfect perception and try to do better on the next one. It seldom occurs to us that it really may have no meaning at all and never was intended to have any, any more than the act of hanging by your feet from parallel bars has any further significance than that you can manage to do it.

So, before retiring to the privacy of our personal couches, let us thank an all wise Providence, that the drama-paradox has passed away.

The Church Supper

THE social season in our city ends up with a bang for the summer when the Strawberry Festival at the Second Congregational Church is over. After that you might as well die. Several people have, in fact.

The Big Event is announced several weeks in advance in that racy sheet known as the "church calendar," which is slipped into the pews by the sexton before anyone has a chance to stop him. There, among such items as a quotation from a recent letter from Mr. and Mrs. Wheelock (the church's missionaries in China who are doing a really splendid work in the face of a shortage of flannel goods), and the promise that Elmer Divvit will lead the Intermediate Christian Endeavor that afternoon, rain or shine, on the subject of "What Can I Do to Increase the Number of Stars in My Crown?" we find the announcement that on Friday night, June the 8th, the Ladies of the Church will unbelt with a Strawberry Festival to be held in the vestry and that, furthermore, Mrs. William Horton MacInting will be at the head of the Committee in Charge. Surely enough good news for one day!

The Committee is then divided into commissary groups, one to provide the short-cake, another to furnish the juice, another the salad, and so on, until everyone has something to do except Mrs. MacInting, the chairman. She agrees to furnish the paper napkins and to send her car around after the contributions which the others are making. Then, too, there is the use of her name.

The day of the festival arrives, bright and rainy. All preparations are made for a cozy evening in defiance of the elements; so when, along about four in the afternoon, it clears and turns into a nice hot day, everyone is caught with rubbers and steamy mackintoshes, to add to the fun. For, by four o'clock in the afternoon, practically everyone in the parish is at the vestry "helping out," as they call it.

"Helping out" consists of putting on an apron over your good clothes, tucking up the real lace cuffs, and dropping plates. The scene in the kitchen of the church at about five-thirty in the afternoon is one to make a prospective convert to Christianity stop and think. Between four and nine thousand women, all wearing aprons over black silk dresses, rush back and forth carrying platters of food, bumping into each other, hysterical with laughter, filling pitchers with hot coffee from a shiny urn, and poking good-natured fun at Mr. Numaly and Mr. Dow, husbands who have been drafted into service and who, amid screams of delight from the ladies, have also donned aprons and are doing the dropping of the heavier plates and ice-cream freezers.

"Look at Mr. Dow!" they cry. "Some good-looking girl you make, Mr. Dow!"

"Come up to my house, Mr. Numaly, and I'll hire you to do our cooking."

"Alice says for Mr. Numaly to come up to her house and she'll hire him as a cook! Alice, you're a caution!"

And so it goes, back and forth, good church-members all, which means that their banter contains nothing off-

104

Mr. Numaly and Mr. Dow are a little fed up with being the center of taunting

color and, by the same token, nothing that was coined later than the first batch of buffalo nickels.

In the meantime, the paying guests are arriving out in the vestry and are sniffing avidly at the coffee aroma, which by now has won its fight with the smell of musty hymn books which usually dominates the place. They leave their hats and coats in the kindergarten room on the dwarfed chairs and wander about looking with week-day detachment at the wall-charts showing the startling progress of the Children of Israel across the Red Sea and the list of gold-star pupils for the month of May. Occasionally they take a peek in at the kitchen and remark on the odd appearance of Messrs. Numaly and Dow, who by this time are just a little fed up on being the center of the taunting and have stopped answering back.

The kiddies, who have been brought in to gorge themselves on indigestible strawberry concoctions, are having a gay time tearing up and down the vestry for the purpose of tagging each other. They manage to reach the door just as Mrs. Camack is entering with a platter full of cabbage salad, and later she explains to Mrs. Reddy while the latter is sponging off her dress that this is the last time she is going to have anything to do with a church supper at which those Basnett children are allowed. The Basnett children, in the meantime, oblivi-ous of this threat, are giving all their attention to slipping pieces of colored chalk from the blackboard into the hot rolls which have just been placed on the tables. And, considering what small children they are, they are doing remarkably well at it.

At last everyone is ready to sit down. In fact, several

invited guests do sit down, and have to be reminded that Dr. Murney has yet to arrange the final details of the supper with Heaven before the chairs can be pulled out. This ceremony, with the gentle fragrance of strawberries and salad rising from the table, is one of the longest in the whole list of church rites; and when it is finally over there is a frantic scraping of chairs and clatter of cutlery and babble of voices which means that the hosts of the Lord have completed another day's work in the vineyard and are ready, nay, willing, to toy with several tons of foodstuffs.

The adolescent element in the church has been recruited to do the serving, but only a few of them show

Turning suddenly and saying, "No coffee, thank you!"

up at the beginning of the meal. The others may be found by any member of the committee frantic enough to search them out, sitting in little groups of two on the stairs leading up to the organ loft or indulging in such forms of young love as tie-snatching and braid-pulling up in the study.

The unattached youths and maids who are induced

to take up the work of pouring coffee do it with a vim but very little skill. Pouring coffee over the shoulder of a person sitting at a long table with dozens of other people is a thing that you ought to practice weeks in advance for, and these young people step right in on the job without so much as a dress rehearsal. The procedure is, or should be, as follows:

Standing directly behind the person about to be served, say in a loud but pleasant voice: "Coffee?" If the victim wishes it, he or she will lift the cup from the table and hold it to be filled, with the left forefinger through the handle and bracing the cup against the right upper-arm. The pourer will then have nothing to do but see to it that the coffee goes from the pitcher to the cup.

Where the inexperienced often make a mistake is in reaching for the cup themselves and starting to pour before finding out if the victim wants coffee. This results in nine cases out of six in the victim's turning suddenly and saying: "No coffee, thank you, please!", jarring the arm of the pourer and getting the coffee on the cuff.

For a long time nothing is heard but the din of religious eating and then gradually, one by one, forks slip from nerveless fingers, chairs are scraped back, and the zealots stir heavily to their feet. All that remains is for the committee to gather up the remains and congratulate themselves on their success.

The next event in the calendar will not be until October, when the Men's Club of the church will prepare and serve a supper of escalloped oysters and hot rolls. Join now and be enrolled for labor in the vineyard in the coming year.

Horse-Sense Editorial

*(In very large type on the first page of your
favorite fiction magazine)*

A MAN walked into my office the other day and
tried to sell me some buttercups.

"Some buttercups, Mr. Blank?" he said, smiling.

"When you say that, smile," I replied. And from the
way I spoke, he knew that I meant what I said.

Now that man went about his job in the wrong way.
Most of us go about our jobs in the wrong way. We
forget the other fellow. They say that an elephant never
forgets. Did you ever hear of an elephant failing in
business? Elephants never forget, and daisies won't tell.
Two things that we humans might well take to heart.

Supposing Moses had forgotten the other fellow. The
great Law-Giver was, above all else, a two-fisted business
man. He knew the rate of exchange, and he knew that
what goes up must come down. Moses was no elephant.
Neither was he a daisy. And yet Moses will be remembered when most of us are forgotten.

The other day I met an old school-mate. He was crying. "Well, old timer," I said, "what's that you've got in
your hand?"

"My other hand," he replied, shaking it.

Now the reason my old school-mate hadn't made good
was that he kept one hand inside the other. He was
drawing on his principal. He had never heard of such
a thing as interest.

A lot of people think interest is a bad thing. They call people who take interest on their money "usurers." And yet Ezra was a "usurer." Job was a "usurer." St. Paul was a "usurer." Samuel M. Vauclain, President of the Baldwin Locomotive Works, is a "usurer." Think that over on your cash register and see if I am not right.

Do you suppose that God sent manna down to the Israelites for nothing? Not much. They paid for it, and they paid for it good. The gold alone in the Ark of the Covenant ran into hundreds of thousands of dollars. Hundreds of thousands of dollars in "interest." Easy come, easy go.

On the street in which I live there is a line of trees. They are fine, big trees, full of twigs and branches. All except one. This one tree has no twigs or branches. It hasn't even any leaves. It just stands there. One day last week I determined to see what was wrong with that tree. I wanted to know why, in a line of fine, strong trees, there should be one weak one. I suspected that it wasn't playing the game right. Not many of us do.

So I went close to it and examined it. It wasn't a tree at all. It was a hydrant.

Watch out that you aren't a hydrant in a line of trees. Or, worse yet, a line of trees in a hydrant.

Chemists' Sporting Extra!

Big Revolutionary Discovery Upsetting Everything

TO APPRECIATE the rapid strides which the science of chemistry has made in the last fifty years all one has to do is to think back on the days when we all, like a lot of poor saps, believed that the molecule was the smallest division into which you could divide matter. Then someone came along and proved that the molecule itself could be divided into something called atoms. Well, the relief we felt at this announcement! Everyone went out and got drunk.

Then came another scientist (he married a Cheever), who said that if you honestly wanted to get down to the fine points of the thing you could divide the atom up into much smaller units. This tiniest of all divisions of matter he called the "electron," after his little daughter Tiny, she being the smallest one in his family.

This seemed to be just about final, for the man said that an electron was a particle of negative electricity (one which knows when to say "No"), and that a "proton" was a particle of positive electricity, and that if you didn't believe it you could go and look for yourself. So it seemed pretty definitely settled that the electron was as small as you could get, and that unless you were crazy you wouldn't ever want to get even *that* small. So people began to put on their coats and hats and started to go back to work.

112

But that just shows. Now comes a Dr. Ernst J. Flazzer, of the University of Carlsbad, who declares that the electron is susceptible of being divided still further, and that, what is more, he has done it, right on his own porch. He calls the new subdivision "traffets," and claims there are eight or ten million of them in one electron.

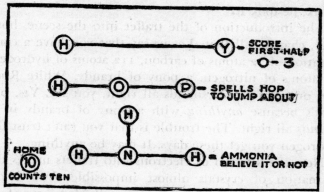

Graphic chart showing the subdivision of hydrogen electrons into serfs, feudal lords and princes. (A.D. 800-A.D. 1200.)

This practically revolutionizes modern chemistry. Modern chemistry has been revolutionized seven times now. The discovery of the traffet means that we shall have to go back over all the researches that we have made in the past fifty years and throw away all that nice stuff in the test tubes.

For instance, in the old days, when you passed an electric current through water (H_2O), the free atoms of oxygen went in one direction and the free atoms of hydrogen went in the opposite one. At the count of ten they were supposed to turn around and see who had gone farthest. This game was called "Peek-o."

It was the same with a gas. A molecule of CO_2 was the seat of such activity and good-natured rivalry on a pleasant day that you could hear the shouts a mile away. *Every* one had a good time in a molecule of CO_2. That was before even electrons were heard of. Just horse-cars. There were no jazz bands, and when any one wanted a drink, he took it.

The introduction of the traffet into the scene, however, changes all that. Let us say that you have a combination of 72 atoms of carbon, 112 atoms of hydrogen, 18 atoms of nitrogen, a pony of brandy, White Rock and orange juice. It sounds all right, you say. Yes, but that's because *anything* with a pony of brandy in it *sounds* all right. The trouble is that you can't trust the hydrogen you get these days. It may be anything.

Now the division of electrons into traffets makes the formation of crystals almost impossible. You know crystals. For while you can pass a colloid (white of an egg, for example) through a parchment paper, a crystalloid (such as pencils) will not go through. This is because the atoms of hydrogen, coming into conjunction with the atoms of oxygen, refuse to go any farther without some assurance that they aren't going to be made suckers of and subdivided again by the next analyst that comes along. You can't blame them.

Lord Kelvin once said that the presence of 1/1000th part of bismuth in copper would reduce its electrical conductivity so as to make it practically useless. A lot of people laughed when Lord Kelvin said this, but now they are laughing out of the other side of their mouths, for, bismuth or no bismuth (see the famous cartoon in *Punch* called "Dropping the Pilot," showing the Iron Chancellor himself being discarded by the young Emperor), the fact remains that during electrolysis you have to be very, very careful about catching cold. Of course, there is always a chance that Dr. Flazzer may not be right, and there may be no such things as "traffets" in an electron. The awful part of it all is, there is no way of ever finding out whether he is right or not. Once you start questioning these things, you end up back in the brute state with no science at all.

How Much Does the Sun Jump?

An Account of the Stroboscope, the New Tell-Tale

THE wonders of our solar universe, and of the thousands and thousands of other universes which we now know dot the heavens, were never more clearly demonstrated than they have been by the recently devised "stroboscope," an invention of Dr. Charles Van Heak, by means of which we are able to measure sun-jumps.

It was not known until recently that the sun jumped at all. It has been known for a long time that the sun is 92,830,000 miles from the earth (except on Leap Year). So much has been an open secret. It has also been recognized in a general way that the moon is swinging at a terrific rate around the sun and that the earth (our Earth) goes back and forth between the sun and the moon once every twenty-four hours, drawing nearest to the sun at noon and then turning back to the moon. This makes our "night" and "day," or, as some say, "right" and "left." Men have also known a long time that if you took a train going a hundred miles an hour you would stand a fat chance of ever reaching the sun.

Our own little colony of stars (we call it "our own," although we just rent it), the Solar System, is composed of millions and millions of things, each one 396,505,-000,000,000 miles away from the others. If you will take your little sister out-of-doors some clear winter's night to look at the stars, and will stand on the top of a high hill from which you can get a good view of the heavens, you will probably both catch very bad colds.

Now it was not known until 1899, when Professor George M. MacRerly began his experiments with gin and absinthe, that the sun was hot at all. One morning, after having been up all night in the laboratory, Prof. MacRerly reached up and touched the sun and was severely burned. He bears the scar to this day. Following this discovery, scientists immediately set about to measure the sun's heat and to see what could be done to stop it. It was during the progress of these experiments that it was found out that the sun jumped.

How, you may say, can we tell that a body 92,000,000 miles away jumps? And, if it does, what the hell difference does it make, anyway? Ninety-two million miles is ninety-two million miles, and we have got enough things within a radius of five miles to worry about without watching the sun jump. This is what people said when Dr. Van Heak began his researches on the subject. A lot of them still say it.

But Dr. Van Heak was not discouraged. He got out an old oblong box, and somewhere found a cover for it. Into this box he put his lunch. Then he went up to his observatory on the roof and sat. When he came down he had worked out a device for measuring sun-jumps, the "stroboscope."

The principle of the "stroboscope" is that of the steam-engine, except that it has no whistle. It is based on the fact that around the sun there is a brilliantly luminous envelope of vaporous matter known as the "chromosphere." We are practically certain that this "chromosphere" exists. If it doesn't, Dr. Van Heak is out of luck, that's all.

Now, knowing that this gas gives off waves of varying lengths, according to the size of the atmosphere, and that these wave lengths can be analyzed by the spectroscope (a wonderful instrument which breaks up wave lengths and plays, "See You in My Dreams" at the same time), Dr. Van Heak has constructed an instrument which will catch these rays as they come from the "chromosphere," spank them soundly, and send them right back again where they belong. Thus, when the sun jumps, if it ever does, the movement, however slight, will be registered on the "stroboscope" by the ringing of a tiny bell, as any deflection of these rays at all will strike the sensitized plate at the top of the instrument and will break it. As it breaks, the bell rings. Thus the observer will know that the sun has jumped.

The next step is to find out some use to which the "stroboscope" can be put.

Looking Shakespeare Over

AT THE end of the current theatrical season, the trustees of the Shakespeare estate will probably get together at the Stratford House and get pie-eyed. It has been a banner year for "the Immortal Bard," as his wife used to call him. Whatever the royalties are that revert to the estate, there will be enough to buy a couple of rounds anyway, and maybe enough left over to hire an entertainer.

There was a time during the winter in New York when you couldn't walk a block without stepping on some actor or actress playing Shakespeare. They didn't all make money, but it got the author's name into the papers, and publicity never hurt anyone, let alone a writer who has been dead three hundred years and whose stuff isn't adaptable for the movies.

The only trouble with acting Shakespeare is the actors. It brings out the worst that is in them. A desire to read aloud the soliloquy (you know the one I mean) is one of the first symptoms a man has that he is going to be an actor. If ever I catch any of my little boys going out behind the barn to recite this speech, I will take them right away to a throat specialist and have their palates removed. One failure is enough in a family.

And then, too, the stuff that Will wrote, while all right to sit at home and read, does *not* lend itself to really snappy entertainment on the modern stage. It takes just

119

about the best actor in the world to make it sound like anything more than a declamation by the young lady representing the Blue and the Gray on Memorial Day. I know that I run counter to many cultured minds in this matter, but I think that, if the truth were known, there are a whole lot more of us who twitch through two-thirds of a Shakespearean performance than the last census would lead one to believe. With a company consisting of one or two stars and the rest hams (which is a good liberal estimate) what can you expect? Even Shakespeare himself couldn't sit through it without reading the ads on the program a little.

But you can't blame the actor entirely. According to present standards of what constitutes dramatic action, most of Will's little dramas have about as much punch as a reading of a treasurer's report. To be expected to thrill over the dramatic situations incident to a large lady's dressing up as a boy and fooling her own husband, or to follow breathlessly a succession of scenes strung together like magic-lantern slides and each ending with a perfectly corking rhymed couplet, is more than ought to be asked of anyone who has, in the same season, seen "Loyalties" or any one of the real plays now running on Broadway.

It is hard to ask an actor to make an exit on a line like:

"I am glad on't: I desire no more delight
    Than to be under sail and gone tonight"

without sounding like one of the characters in Palmer Cox's Brownies saying:

"And thus it was the Brownie Band,
    Came tumbling into Slumberland."

That is why they always have to exit laughingly in a Shakespearean production. The author has provided them with such rotten exits. If they don't do something —laugh, cry, turn a handspring, or something—they are left flat in the middle of the stage with nothing to do but say: "Well, I must be going." In "The Merchant of Venice," the characters are forced to keep up a running fire of false-sounding laughter to cover up the artificial nature of what they have just said:

"At the park gate, and therefore haste away
  For we must measure twenty miles today. A-ha-
  ha-ha-ha-ha!" (Off l. c.)

To hear *Lorenzo* and *Gratiano* walking off together you would have thought that *Lorenzo* had the finest line of funny stories in all Venice, so loud and constantly did they laugh, whereas, if the truth were known, it was simply done to save their own and Shakespeare's face. Now my contention is that any author who can't get his stuff over on the stage without making the actors do contortions, is not so good a playwright technically as Eugene Walters is. And now for the matter of comedy.

An actor, in order to get Shakespeare's comedy across, has got to roll his eyes, rub his stomach, kick his father in the seat, make his voice crack, and place his finger against the side of his nose. There is a great deal of talk about the vulgarity and slap-stick humor of the movies. If the movies ever tried to put anything over as horsy and crass as the scene in which young *Gobbo* kids his blind father, or *Falstaff* hides in the laundry hamper, there would be sermons preached on it in pulpits all over the country. It is impossible for a good actor, as we know good actors today, to handle a Shakespearean low comedy part, for it demands mugging and tricks which no good actor would permit himself to do. If Shakespeare were alive today and writing comedy for the movies, he would be the head-liner in the Mack Sennett studios. What he couldn't do with a cross-eyed man!

Another thing which has made the enjoyment of Shakespeare on the stage a precarious venture for this section of the theatre-going public at least, is the thoroughness with which the schools have desiccated his works. In "The Merchant of Venice," for example, there was hardly a line spoken which had not been so diagnosed by English teachers from the third grade up that it had lost every vestige of freshness and grace which it may once have had. Every time I changed schools, I ran into a class which was just taking up "The Merchant of Venice." Consequently, I learned to hate every word of the play. When *Bassanio* said:

"Which makes her seat of Belmont Colchis' strand,
And many Jasons come in quest of her"

in my mind there followed a chorus of memories of questions asked by Miss Mergatroid, Miss O'Shea, Miss Twitchell, Mr. Henby, and Professor Greenally, such as: "Now what did Shakespeare mean by 'Colchis strand'?" "Can anyone in the room tell me why Portia's lovers were referred to as 'Jasons'? Robert Benchley, I wonder if you can leave off whispering to Harold Bemis long enough to tell me what other Portia in history is mentioned in this passage?"

Perhaps that is the whole trouble with Shakespeare anyway. Too many people have taken him up. If they

122

would let you alone, to read snatches from his plays now and then when you wanted to, and *stop* reading when you wanted to, it might not be so bad. But no! They must ask you what he meant by this, and where the inflection should come on that, and they must stand up in front of scenery and let a lot of hams declaim at you while you are supposed to murmur "Gorgeous!" and "How well he knew human nature!" as if you couldn't go to Bartlett's "Quotations" and get the meat of it in half the time. I wouldn't be surprised, if things keep on as they are, if Shakespeare began to lose his hold on people. I give him ten centuries more at the outside.

Evolution Sidelights

Showing Nature's Way of Taking Care of Her Young

ONE of the most fascinating chapters in the story of Evolution is that in which we see animals of a certain type change, through the ages, into animals of quite a different type, through a process of the survival of the fittest and adaptation to environment. These are pretty big words, I am afraid, but before we are through you will see what they mean, or you will take a sock on the nose.

Thus we learn that our present-day sheep, from whose warm blanket our silk socks are made, was once, in the early, early days of the earth, a member of the hermit-crab family. It was during the Palæozoic Age, before the great glaciers had swept down over the land leaving their trail of empty tins and old shoes, even before the waters had receded from the earth. So you can see how long ago it was! Just years and years.

Well, anyway, the hermit-crab of the Palæozoic Era lived in the slime and sulked. He didn't like being a hermit-crab. He didn't see any future in it. And, as the sun beat down on the earth, and the waters gradually receded, the crab was left high and dry on the beach and little Palæozoic children built forts on him. This got him pretty sore.

Now as the centuries went by and the sun continued to beat down on the earth, the color of the mud changed

124

from reddish brown to a dirty gray. Formerly, the crabs who were reddish brown had been more or less hidden in the reddish-brown mud, but now they stood out like a rainy Thursday, and it was the dirty-gray crabs who were protected from the onslaughts of the hordes of crab-devouring mantes which came down from the mountains. Gradually the red crabs became extinct, and the gray crabs, through their protective coloring, survived. The red crabs that you see today are a new batch, and anyway, don't ask questions.

The next step was ages and ages later, when the crab, in order to get food, began to stretch himself out to get to the grass which grew up along the edge of the beach. He also wanted to take a crack at this running business he had heard so much about. So, in another hundred million years, or, at any rate, a good long time, these crabs had developed teeth with which to pull up grass and chew it, and four legs on which to run. By this time it was late in April.

We finally see these four-legged herbivorous crabs who had managed to survive the rigors of the seasons, running, as sheep will, farther and farther north, where the weather grew colder and colder. This made it necessary for them to develop some protective covering, and those lucky crabs who were able to work themselves up into a sort of wool were the ones who stood the climate. The others froze to death and became soldiers' monuments.

And that is how Nature took care of the hermit-crab and turned him into a sheep.

The same thing happens right under our very eyes today, only quicker. Nature has endowed certain animals with the power to change color at a second's notice, and thus elude pursuers. Of course, a simpler way for such animals would be to stay in the house all the time and make faces out the window at their enemies, but some of them, like the horse, simply have to go out-of-doors occasionally on business, and it is then that their ability to change coloring comes in so handy.

Having taken the horse as an example, we may as well continue. Professor Rossing, in his book, "Animal, Vegetable or Mineral?" reports a case of a man who was chasing a bay mare to try to make her eat her breakfast. He had chased her all around the yard, both of them laughing so hard they could scarcely run. Suddenly, the mare, deciding that there had been enough of this foolishness, drew up alongside a red-brick silo, and ducking her head slightly, changed coloring in an instant, taking on exactly the shade and markings of the brick surface. Her pursuer was dumbfounded, thinking that the mare had disappeared into thin air. As he drew near to the silo, to examine what he felt sure must be a trap-door in the side, the mare romped away again, startling him so that he dropped the feed-bag, and the chase was over. The mare, with Nature's aid, had won. How many of us can say the same?

Teaching the Old
Idea to Skate

THEY told me that once you had skated, you never forgot how. It was like swimming, they said. I knew, of course, that *that* wasn't so. Skating is nothing like swimming. But as I thought back on the days, ten years ago, when I used to glide easily over the lumpy surface of the Charles, it did seem plausible that some of the old facility had remained, even after all these years.

I never was what you would call a fancy skater, even in my heyday. None of my attempts at cutting numerals or weaving backward ever quite came off. I had the idea all right, and would start off rather finely, perhaps too finely, but at the turn something usually went wrong and I became discouraged, and while I seldom actually fell, it might have been more impressive if I had. A good, resounding fall is no disgrace. It is the fantastic writhing to avoid a fall which destroys any illusion of being a gentleman. How like life that is, after all!

On a good straightaway, however, I had always been able to make a respectable progress, nothing flashy but good, solid plodding, with a liberal swinging of the arms to add propulsion power which sometimes carried me along at what I flattered myself was a tremendous rate of speed. As I looked back on this accomplishment, it did not seem over-confidence on my part to agree to join my little boy in a frolic on the ice.

The pond was thronged with intensely young people.

This in itself was disheartening. The girls, arrayed in knickerbockers, looked as if they would enjoy hugely anything that I might do in the way of acrobatics, and the boys were offensively proficient. They seemed to be oblivious of the fact that I was a good competent skater when they were having trouble digesting their first carrots. And they were all so good-looking and well dressed. I was on the point of turning back then and there. I felt that my old blue track-sweater looked very seedy. And the funny thing is that it *did.*

I discovered that it was not a strap-end but my forefinger

However, I had my pride and my little boy's pride in his father which I somehow felt demanded that I go through with the thing. Just how I reasoned it out that making a display of myself on the ice was going to bolster up the family pride, I don't know. Somehow it seemed the thing to do at the time, as the drunk said when asked why he deliberately put his fist through the plate-glass window.

Getting the skates on was not so simple a matter as I remembered it as being, especially as my hands got much colder than they used to in the old days. I worked for some time trying to slip a strap-end under the buckle before I discovered that it was not a strap-end at all but my forefinger. By the time I was firmly shod, I was chilled through and felt a little grippy. Then I stood up.

The sensation was similar to that of mounting a horse

There was a sickening lack of stability

for the first time. I was incredibly high up in the air. I looked to the right, expecting to see Long Island Sound over the tree-tops, but the day was not clear enough. There was a sickening lack of stability about everything below my knees and I suddenly realized that my ankles were resting on the ice. There ahead of me stretched a glassy expanse, with my little boy shivering and urging me on. The young people seemed to have stopped their

129

grace of romping and stood watching me. A tinkling girlish laugh rang out on the frosty air, followed by a "sh-h-h-h!" Very well, I would show them.

So, gathering myself like a panther for a spring, I straightened up my ankles, clenched my fists, gave a powerful swing with my arms, and, with head bent low, pushed off with my right foot into a slow, gliding stroke which carried me easily out to the middle of the pond.

"Come along, son," I called back, "follow Daddy!"

Cleaning Out the Desk

THE first thing that I have got to do in my campaign to make this bright new year a better one for all of us is to clean out my desk. I started on this a little over a week ago, but so far, I have got only to the second drawer on the left hand side. I think that people must have been sneaking up during the last three or four years and putting things in my desk drawers while I have been asleep (they couldn't have done it while I was awake, for I have been working here every minute and would most certainly have noticed them at it, that is, unless they were dressed like gnomes. I never pay any attention to gnomes fussing around my desk when I am working. In fact, I rather like it). But somebody has been at work, and hard at work, putting little objects and bits of paper in my desk drawers since the last time I went through them. And I don't know whether to throw them away or not.

For instance, what would I ever have wanted with an old mitten that I should have tucked it 'way back in that upper left hand drawer? It was right up against the back partition of the drawer, under a program of the six-day bicycle race of February, 1933, and clinging to it, almost a part of it, was half a Life-Saver (clove flavor). Now, I never wear mittens, and even if I did it certainly wouldn't be a mitten like this. Furthermore, it has no mate. I haven't tried it on, for I would rather not have

131

much to do with it in its present state, but I think it is for the right hand only. As I lift it gingerly out of the drawer (I was at first afraid that it was a small beaver) it seems to have some lumpy object tucked away up in the very tip, but I am not going in to find out what it is. I may have a man come up with a ferret and get the whole thing settled once and for all, but for the present both the mitten and the piece of Life-Saver are over in the corner of the room where I tossed them. I almost wish that they were back in the drawer again.

Just in front of the mitten, and a little to the left, I came upon a pile of old check book stubs (1936-'38 inclusive, with February, April, July and August of 1936, and September to December of 1937 missing). On thumbing these over I was fascinated to see how many checks I had made out to "cash" and for what generous amounts. I must have been a pretty prodigal boy in those days. Dear me, dear me! Here is one made out to the Alsatian Novelty Company for $11.50 on Oct. 5, 1936. What traffic was I having with the Alsatian Novelty Company, do you suppose? Whatever it was, it wasn't enough of a novelty to make much impression on me—or on any one else, I guess. Maybe it was that rubber girdle that I sent for when I first began to notice that I was putting on weight. Whatever became of that, I wonder? I know what became of the weight, because it is right there where it was, but the girdle never did much but make me look bulky. Maybe the girdle is in the bottom drawer which I haven't come to yet.

Now about those old check stubs. I suppose that they might as well be thrown away, but then supposing the Alsatian Novelty Company should come around and say

132

that I never paid the $11.50! I would be in a pretty pickle, wouldn't I? Of course, no jury would acquit me merely on the evidence of a check stub, but I don't know where the cancelled checks are and this would at least show that I was systematic about the thing. Then, too, the income tax people never get around to complaining about your payments until three or four years after they are made, and it might come in handy to be able to write them and say: "On March 15, 1938, according to my records, sent you a check for $45.60. It is up to you to find it." It might frighten them a little, anyway. So I guess the best thing to do is to put the stubs right back in the drawer and sit tight. All I hope is that no trouble arises over the checks drawn during those months which are lost. I wouldn't have a leg to stand on in that case.

In with the pile of check stubs I found a pamphlet entitled, "The Control of the Root Knot," issued by the U. S. Department of Agriculture in 1933. Now "root knot" is a thing that I never have had much trouble with (knock wood) and why I should have been saving a pamphlet on its control for seven years is something that not only mystifies, but irritates me a little. I read some of it and even then I didn't see why.

However, in 1933 I evidently thought that it might come in handy someday, and if I throw it away now it would be just my luck to come down with root knot next week and need it very badly. It is possible, of course, that I never had any hand in sending for the pamphlet at all and that it has been put in my desk by those mysterious agencies which I suspected at first (gnomes, or people representing themselves to be gnomes), in which case I am just making a fool of myself by hoarding it for another seven years. I guess that I will put it aside and read it thoroughly some day before throwing it away. Maybe my name is mentioned in it somewhere.

One article, however, which I recognized almost immediately is an old German pipe, one of those with a long, hooked stem and a bowl covered with straw. I think that I bought that myself; at any rate I remember

trying to smoke it once or twice. But as soon as I got the tobacco into it and the fire started so that it would draw, it went out. This, I figured, was owing to my shutting the lid down over the bowl. The lid was evidently meant to be shut down, as there was a hinge on it (now fortunately broken so that it hangs loosely to one side), but I guess that I didn't quite have the knack of the thing, I remember thinking that sometime I might want to dress up in German costume for a lark or something, and then if I saved the pipe all I would have to get would be the German costume. So I saved it, and,

as luck would have it, have never been called upon to
dress up. There is still some of the original tobacco in
it—some is in it and some is in the drawer—and I got
a little sentimental over the memories of the old days
in Munich where I bought it. (I was in Munich for
three hours, between trains.) I even tried to smoke a
little of it without clamping down the lid, but either
the tobacco wasn't very good or my stomach isn't what
it used to be, for I didn't go through with the scheme.
"Wer nicht die Sehnsucht kennt——" and whatever the
rest of the quotation is.

All of this, you will see, took up quite a lot of time.
It is necessary that I get the desk cleaned out if I am
ever going to start fresh now, but, with the first two
drawers giving up such a wealth of sentimental memo-
rabilia, I must evidently give over several days to it.
There is, for instance, the letter from my insurance company, dated June 15, 1938, saying that as I have allowed
policy No. 4756340 to lapse it will be necessary for me
to take another physical examination before I can be
reinstated. Now the question arises: Did I ever take the
examination, and am I reinstated? I remember taking
an examination, but I think it was for the war. I certainly
don't think that I have had my shirt off before a doctor
since 1938 and I am afraid that if I call them up about
it to find out they will make me do it right away, and
that would be too bad because I wouldn't get anywhere
near such a good mark now as I would have when the
policy first lapsed. I might even have to do a lot of home-
work in order to catch up with my class. I think what I
will do is set about right now getting into condition

135

again and then call them up. I don't see how that letter ever got so far back in the drawer.

There is one thing, however, that I shall never be short of again, and that is matches. I have never seen so many matches in one place as there were in my desk drawer. Here I have sat day after day, unable to work because I was out of matches with which to light my pipe, and all the time there were enough matches right under my nose (if I had put my nose in the upper left hand drawer) to do parlor tricks with for 10 years. They are all in those little paper covers, some containing five matches, some none, but, added together, a magnificent hoard. I don't right now see the advantage of saving empty match covers, but I suppose I had some good reason at the time. Perhaps I liked the pictures on them. There are some with pictures of hotels on them which I have never visited in my life (Atlantic City has a marvellous representation) and I am afraid that I would have a difficult time denying that I had ever been to the Five Devils Inn in Tia Juana with such damning evidence as two match covers bearing its advertisement staring the examiners in the face. But honestly, I haven't. However, there are seven matches left in one and one match in the other; so I am going to save them anyway. And what a lot of fun I am going to have with my new-found treasure! It might even be the means of my becoming a pyromaniac.

But there! I mustn't think of such things now. All I have to do is get those other four drawers cleaned out and the papers which are on the back of my desk sorted out (I am a little nervous about tackling those papers, as I have heard a strange rustling in there lately and there might be field mice) and I shall be all spick and span and ready for the new year. All I hope is that the other drawers don't take as long as the first two have, or it will be 1941, and then I would have to wait until 1950 for another good, even year to start fresh.

Carnival Week in Sunny Las Los

YOU have all doubtless wanted to know, at one time or another, a few of the quaint customs which residents of the continent of Europe seem to feel called upon to perpetuate from one century to another. You may know about a few of them already, such as childbearing (which has been taken up on this continent to such an alarming extent) and others of the more common variety of folk mannerisms, but I am very proud and happy to be able to tell you today of some of the less generally known customs of the inhabitants of that medieval Spanish province Las Los (or Los Las, as it was formerly called, either way meaning "The The" *pl.*) where I have had the extremely bad fortune to be spending the summer.

Las Los, nestling, as it does, in the intercostal nooks of the Pyrenees, makes up into one of the nicest little plague-spots on the continent of Europe. Europe has often claimed that Las Los was *not* a part of it, and in 1356 Spain began a long and costly war with France, the loser to take Los Las and two outfielders. France won and Spain built an extension onto the Pyrenees in which to hide Los Las. They succeeded in hiding it from view, but there was one thing about Los Las that they forgot; so you always know that it is there.

It was in this little out-of-the-way corner of the world, then, that I set up my easel and began painting my

138

fingers and wrists. I soon made friends with the natives (all of whom were named Pedro) and it was not long before they were bringing me their best Sunday knives and sticking them in my back for me to try and tell which was which. And such laughter would go up when I guessed the wrong one! All Latins, after all, are just children at heart.

But I am not here to tell you of the many merry days I myself spent in Las Los, but of some of the native customs which I was privileged to see, and, once in a while, take part in. They rather resent an outsider taking part in most of them, however, for there is an old saying in Las Los that "when an outsider takes part, rain will surely dart" (meaning "dart" from the clouds, you see) and above all things rain is abhorred in that section of the country, as rain has a tendency to cleanse whatever it touches, and, as another old proverb has it, "clean things, dead things"—which isn't exactly accurate, but appeals to these simple, childish people, to whom cleanliness is next to a broken hip.

First of all, then, let us tiptoe up on the natives of Las Los during their carnival time. The carnival week comes during the last week in July, just when it is hottest. This makes it really ideal for the Los Lasians, for extreme heat, added to everything else, renders their charming little town practically unbearable. This week was chosen many hundreds of years ago and is supposed to mark the anniversary of the marriage of old Don Pedro's daughter to a thunderbolt, a union which was so unsatisfactory to the young lady that she left her husband in two days and married a boy named Carlos, who sold tortillas. This so enraged the thunderbolt that

139

he swore never to come to Los Las again, and, from that day to this (so the saying goes, I know not whether it be true or not) that region has never had any locusts. (This would almost make it seem that the repulsed bridegroom had been a locust, but the natives, on being questioned, explain that the *patois* for "thunderbolt" [*enjuejoz*] is very much like the *patois* for "locust" [*enjuejoz*] and that the thunder god, in giving his order for the future of Los Las, put the accent on the wrong syllable and cut them off from locusts instead of thunderstorms). This may, or may not, be the truth, but, as I said to the old man who told me "Who the hell cares?" The first day of the Carnival of the Absence of Locusts (just why they should be so cocky about having no locusts is not clear. Locusts would be a god-send compared to some of the things they *have* got) is spent in bed, storing up strength for the festival. On this day all the shops, except those selling wine, are closed. This means that a little shop down by the river which sells sieves is closed. People lie in bed and send out to the wine-shops for the native drink, which is known as *wheero*. All that is necessary to do with this drink is to place it in an open saucer on the window sill and inhale deeply from across the room. In about eight seconds the top of the inhaler's head rises slowly and in a dignified manner until it reaches the ceiling where it floats, bumping gently up and down. The teeth then drop out and arrange themselves on the floor to spell "Portage High School, 1930," the eyes roll upward and backward, and a strange odor of burning rubber fills the room. This is followed by an unaccountable feeling of intense lassitude.

140

"For the love of God, shut up that incessant banging!"

Thus we may expect nothing from the natives for the first two days of the carnival, for the second day is spent in looking for bits of head and teeth, and in general moaning. (A sorry carnival, you will say—and *I* will say, too.) But later on, things will brighten up.

On the third day the inhabitants emerge, walking very carefully in order not to jar off their ears, and get into a lot of decorated ox carts. They are not very crazy about getting into these ox carts, but it is more or less expected of them at carnival time. Pictures are taken of them riding about and are sent to the London illustrated papers, and if they were to pass up one year without riding in decorated ox carts, it wouldn't seem like carnival week to the readers of the London illustrated papers. You can hardly blame a man with a *wheero* hangover, however, for not wanting to bump around over cobblestones in an old two-wheeled cart, even if it has got paper flowers strung all over it. One of the saddest sights in the world is to see a native, all dressed up in red and yellow, with a garland of orange roses around his neck, jolting and jouncing along over hard stone bumps with a girl on his knee, and trying to simulate that famous Spanish smile and gay abandon, all the time feeling that one more bump and away goes that meal he ate several days ago, along with his legs and arms and portions of his lower jaw. No wonder Spaniards look worried.

However, there is a great deal of shouting and cawing among those who can open their mouths, and occasionally someone hits a tambourine. This is usually frowned upon by the person standing next to the tambourine-hitter and a remark, in Spanish, is made which could roughly be translated as: "For the love of God, shut up that incessant banging!"

The carnival, which is known as *Romeria*, is supposed to be a festival of the picnic type combined with a religious pilgrimage to some sort of shrine. This shrine, however, is never reached, as along about noon of the third day some desperate guy, with a hangover no longer to be borne, evolves a cure on the "hair of the dog that bit you" theory, and the *wheero* is brought out again. The village watering trough is filled with it and a sort of native dance is held around the trough, everyone inhaling deeply. Those who are still unable to inhale are carried to the edge of the trough and a little *wheero* is rubbed on their upper-lips, just under the nose. Then it is "good-night all, and a merry, merry trip to Blanket Bay," for the festive villagers, and the carnival is shot to hell. A week later business is quietly resumed.

On the fifth day of the carnival there is supposed to be a bull chase through the streets. The principle of the thing is that a bull is let loose and everyone chases it, or vice versa. As, however, there was nobody fit to chase a butterfly, much less a bull, on the fifth day of this carnival, I had to take care of the bull myself. The two of us sat all alone in the public square among the cadavers drinking a sort of lemon squash together.

"A dash of *wheero*?" I asked the bull.

Well, you should have heard him laugh! After that, I got up on his back and rode all around the town, visiting the points of interest and climbing several of the better-looking mountains. Pretty soon we were in Turkey, where we saw many interesting sights and then, swinging around through the Balkans, I got back just in time for me to scramble into bed. I must have hit my head on the footboard while pulling up the sheet, for the next morning (or whenever it was) when I awoke, I had quite a bad headache. Thank heaven I knew enough to lay off that *wheero*, however. I'm no fool.

Another Uncle Edith Christmas Story

UNCLE Edith said: "I think it is about time that I told you a good old-fashioned Christmas story about the raging sea."

"Aw, nuts!" said little Philip.

"As you will," said Uncle Edith, "but I shall tell it just the same. I am not to be intimidated by a three-year-old child. Where was I?"

"You were over backwards, with your feet in the air, if I know anything about you," said Marian, who had golden hair and wore it in an unbecoming orange ribbon.

"I guess that you probably are right," said Uncle Edith, "although who am I to say? Anyway, I *do* know that we sailed from Nahant on the fourteenth March."

"What are you—French?" asked little Philip, "the fourteenth March."

"The fourteenth *of* March, then," said Uncle Edith, "and if you don't shut up I will keep right on with the story. You can't intimidate me."

146

"Done and done," said little Philip, who bled quite a lot from a wound in his head inflicted a few seconds before by Uncle Edith.

"We set sail from Nahant on the fourteenth *of* March (nya-a-a-a-a) on the good ship *Patience W. Littbaum,* with a cargo of old thread and bound for Algeciras."

"End of story!" announced Marian in a throaty baritone.

"It is *not* the end of the story, and I will sue anyone who says that it is," petulated Uncle Edith. "You will know well enough when I come to the end of the story, because I shall fall over on my face. Now be quiet or Uncle Edith will give you a great big abrasion on the forehead."

"I can hardly wait," said little Philip, or whichever the hell one of those children it was, I can't keep them all straight, they are all so much alike.

"Aboard," continued Uncle Edith, "aboard were myself, as skipper——"

"Skippered herring," (*a whisper*).

"——Lars Jannssenn, first mate; Max Schnirr, second mate; Enoch Olds, third base; and a crew of seven whose names you wouldn't recognize. However, there we were.

"The first 709 days were uneventful. The sailmaker (a man by the name of Sailmaker, oddly enough) made eleven sails, but, as we had no more ships to put them on, and as our sails were O. K., we had to throw them overboard. This made the men discontented, and there were rumors of mutiny. I sent a reporter up to see the men, however, and the rumors were unconfirmed; so I killed the story. NO MUTINY was the head I put on

147

it in the ship's paper that night, and everybody was satisfied."

"You great big wonderful animal," said Marian, running her tiny hand through Uncle Edith's hair.

"It was nothing," said Uncle Edith, and everybody agreed that it certainly was.

Max Schnirr, second mate

"However," continued the old salt pork, "everyone on board felt that something was wrong. We were at that time at Lat. seventy-eight, Long. seventy-eight, which cancelled each other, making us right back where we started from——"

"Don't tell me that we are back at Nahant again," said little Philip, throwing up.

"Not exactly Nahant," said Uncle Edith, "but within hailing distance of a Nahanted ship."

"You just used Nahant in the first place so that you could pull that gag," said Primrose, who, up to this

148

time, had taken no part in the conversation, not having been born.

"So help me God," said Uncle Edith, "it came to me like *that!*" And he snapped a finger, breaking it. "The ha'nted ship lay just off our starboard bow, and seemed to be manned by mosquitoes. As we drew alongside, however, we found that there was not a soul on board. Not a soul on board."

"That is the second time you have said that," said little whatever-his-name-is—Philip.

Uncle Edith made no reply other than to throw nasty little Philip into irons.

" 'Prepare to board!' was the order given. And everybody, ignoring the chance for a pun, prepared to board the derelict. In a few seconds we were swarming over the side of the empty ship and searching every nook and cranny of her. The search, however, was fruitless. The ship's log was found in the wheelhouse, but, as the last entry read, 'Fair and warm. Billy said he didn't love me as much as he does Anna' we discarded that as evidence. In the galley we found a fried egg, done on only one side, and an old bo'sun who was no good to anybody. Other than these two things, the mystery was complete."

"Not that I give a damn," said Marian, "but what was the explanation to this almost complete mystery?"

"If you will shut your trap," said Uncle Edith, "I will tell you. As I may not have told you, the mystery ship was full of sleeping Hessian troops, such as were used against the colonists in the Revolutionary War. They were very gay in their red coats and powdered wigs, and, had they been awake, might have offered some solution of the problem which now presented itself to us.

"'What shall I do, cap'n?' asked Lars Jannssenn, who had been promoted to purser.

"'What would you *like* to do, Lars?' I asked him.

"'Me, I would like to have three wishes,' was the typically Scandinavian reply. (Lars had belonged to the Scandi-navy before he joined up with us.)

"'They are yours,' I said, more on the spur of the moment than anything else. 'You take your three wishes and put them in your hat and pull it down over your ears. Anybody else?'

"Suddenly there was a scream from below decks. I have heard screams in my day, but never anything like this one. It was dark by now, and there were a lot of couples necking in the lifeboats. But this scream was

Big Executive

(From the Paramount picture "The Man's Angle")

(From the Paramount picture "Controlling the Nerves")

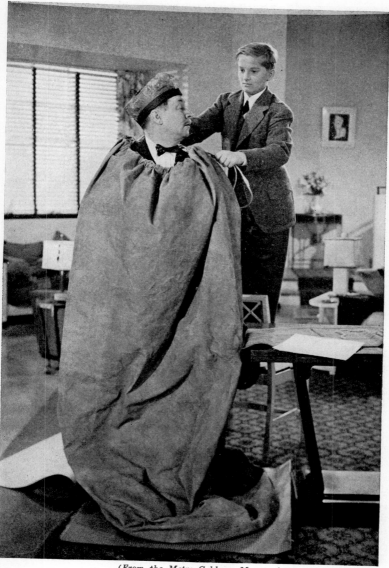

(From the Metro-Goldwyn-Mayer picture "Dark Magic")

Trying On for Size

(From the Metro-Goldwyn-Mayer picture "How to Start the Day")

One . . . Two . . . Three . . . Bend!

Self-Assurance

(*From the Paramount picture "The Witness"*)

(From the Metro-Goldwyn-Mayer picture "How to Sleep")

Position No. 6. Ecstatic

Mens Sana in Corpore Sano

(From the Metro-Goldwyn-Mayer picture "Home Early")

(From the Metro-Goldwyn-Mayer picture "An Hour for Lunch")

Anti-Social

JOHN'S BARBER

(From the Metro-Goldwyn-Mayer picture "An Hour for Lunch")

Frustration

(From the Metro-Goldwyn-Mayer picture "How to Sleep")

Do Not Disturb

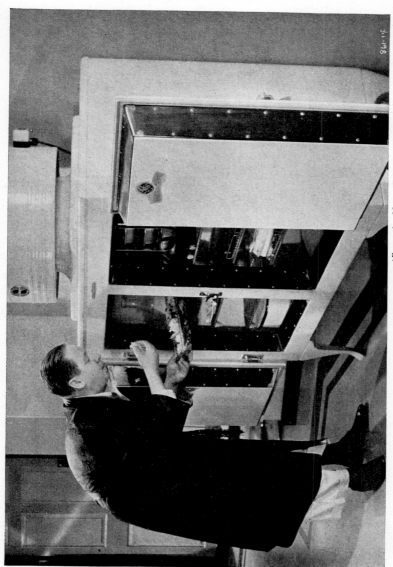

(From the Metro-Goldwyn-Mayer picture "How to Sleep")

The Midnight Snack

(*From the Metro-Goldwyn-Mayer picture "How to Watch Football"*)

The Football Fan

(From the Paramount picture "Keeping in Shape")

Easy Two Hands or The Man Doesn't Know His Own Strength

(From the Paramount picture "The Witness")

Le Demi-Penseur

(From the Metro-Goldwyn-Mayer picture "Dark Magic")

"Yours of the 18th Inst. received and contents noted"

(From the Paramount picture "The Trouble with Husbands")

"I'll be down in just a minute!"

different. It was like nothing human. It came from the bowels of the ship, and you know that's bad.

" 'All hands below!' I cried, and just as everybody was rushing down the hatchways there came a great explosion, seemingly from the jib.

" 'All hands to the jib!' I cried in my excitement.

" 'What is all this—a game?' asked the crew, as one man.

" 'I am captain here,' I said, boxing the compass roundly, 'and what I say goes! In the future please try to remember that fact.'

"Well, this sort of thing went on for hours. Up and down the ship we went, throwing overboard Hessians in our rush, until finally the cook came to me and said: 'Cap'n, I frankly am sick of this. Are there, or are there not, any reasons why we should be behaving like a pack of schoolboys?'

"This was a poser. I called the crew together and we

decided to go back to the *Patience W. Littbaum*. But, on looking over the side, we found a very suspicious circumstance. *The Patience W. Littbaum was gone!*"

"I don't believe it!" said little Philip, from the brig.

Uncle Edith turned sharply. "I thought you were in irons," he said.

"You think a lot," replied little Philip, and the entire casino burst into a gale of laughter, although it was a pretty lousy come-back, even for a three-year-old.

"Very well, then," said Uncle Edith. "I am sorry if you feel that way. For I was just going to end the story by saying that we sailed the mystery ship back to Nahant.

"And where does Christmas come in?" piped up Marian, who hadn't heard a word of Uncle Edith's story.

"Who the hell said anything about Christmas?" asked Uncle Edith in a rage.

And who the hell did?

Community Singing[*]

WITH all the good will which threatens to be abroad in the world during the coming year I am afraid that it looks like a big year for community singing. I don't know why I have this feeling. It is a presentiment such as I have on damp days when my wrists start aching and I know that I am in for a touch of my arthritis. We are going to have a year of community singing, and we are going to have it good.

You may think that I am just an old alarmist, predicting all this before a note has really been sung or even before notices have been sent out for people to get together and start humming. "Wait until they begin to sing," you may say. "Then will be plenty of time to get disagreeable." But I want to be disagreeable now, and I have every reason in the world to be. Certain documents have come to my hand which put things in an even blacker light than I have indicated. Without wishing to be a wet blanket, let me tell you what is already lined up in the way of community singing for the coming season.

Some travel bureau, with a mistaken idea of being alluring, has issued a pamphlet telling on just what dates you can get in on a good community sing. According to this schedule, if you hurry you can just make the musical festival in Dublin of Feis Ceoil (All Ireland), at which I imagine a great deal of tenor will be sung. Or, on Aug. 8, you can catch the Welsh national *eistedd-*

[*] Only nostalgia can be evoked by Mr. Benchley's sensitive discussion of folkways practised in a time when traveling didn't necessarily rate a headline.—Editor's Note.

153

fod, which is to be held at Llanelly. This means singing, if I know anything about the Welsh. I am not quite sure about how to get to Llanelly, but I suppose you take a car marked "Llanelly" and ask the conductor where the *eisteddfod* is being held. He and the motorman will probably sing the directions to you.

Not only are the British Isles threatened with countless get-together sings, smaller than the *feis ceoil* and the *eisteddfod,* but our own dear land is already beginning to blow its pitch pipes in preparation for a year of song and little committees are springing up everywhere to send out postal cards and get all available larynxes lined up for service. Once these things start they sweep the country like wildfire. Remember how quickly that parrots' disease spread. (By the way, were those parrots ever deported or are they still going about the streets in droves endangering the lives of the nation?)

Community singing wouldn't be so bad if it really were community singing. But there are always several people (usually those who get the movement started) who do all the singing, or rather who do the loudest singing, and the rest of the community just stand around holding sheets of music and making low noises in their throats. The loud singers are usually sopranos and are big women who wear black jet beads. If they are not leading the thing completely, they dominate the chorus so that nobody else can make himself heard. No matter how domineering a basso may be, he can't really drown out the rest, owing to the nature of bass singing itself. If you try to sing bass too loud your nose starts bleeding or your chin gets caught down in your collar and you choke to death (to the great satisfaction of everybody).

154

Altos suffer from the same handicap, while tenors are usually of a mild and retiring nature and not given to masterful hogging of sound waves. It is the sopranos that you have to look out for.

Of course, underneath all this bitterness on my part you will detect that I have personal feeling against some soprano who has drowned me out at some time or other. I like to sing (in a group) and, if I am fairly sure of

my part, I like to be heard. In fact, I have been known to go out of my way to make myself heard. But I can't buck a soprano. I have even gone so far as to give up singing in mixed groups for this very reason. In a crowd of men I can hold my own, and frequently do, but in competition with large ladies wearing black jet beads I am frankly outclassed. And I resent it.

There are certain kinds of group singing which are a great help to community, or party, spirit. Those little extemporaneous outbursts around a piano, for which postcards do not have to be sent out and which develop naturally when some one comes across a pile of old music after dinner, are really the most satisfactory of all. That is, they are satisfactory for those who happen to be around the piano singing. The rest of the people in the room are not likely to be so enthusiastic about it. I guess there are no looks so ugly as those shot at a little band of amateur singers by the people in other parts of the room who want to be talking or who are not interested in recalling songs of yesteryear.

But even in the little groups themselves there is likely to spring up some hard feeling, owing to one or two of the group being quicker than the rest to get their particular songs on the rack in front of the pianist. Everyone, when old songs are being dragged out, has his favorites, either for sentimental reasons or because he happens to know all the words. And, if some one else happens to beat you to it in suggesting the number to be tried next, you are likely to stand in silence waiting for them to finish so that you can rush your own choice into the arena. This makes for bad team work and sometimes it happens that the only one singing is the one who has just won the toss.

"Remember this?" some one will shout (the affair reaches the shouting stage very early in the game). And he will begin, in a loud voice, to sing "Call Me up Some Rainy Afternoon," both verses and two choruses. There will be perhaps two others who know a few of the words to "Call Me up Some Rainy Afternoon" and they will join in with something of a will, but those who are too young ever to have known it or who never liked it anyway assume a patently false politeness and wait, looking

But even in the little groups themselves there is likely to spring up
some hard feeling

about the room, for the "Call Me up Some Rainy After-noon" devotees to finish.

Then there is a babel of:

"Remember 'Pony Boy, Pony Boy, won't you be my ——' "

"No, no, this, 'Oh, the moon shines bright tonight upon ——' "

"No, no! Remember 'Lindy, Lindy, sweet as the sug ——' "

"Here's one! 'Dinah, is there any one finer?' " (This from one of the younger members of the group who is thoroughly disgusted with the old boys who are insisting on singing songs he never even knew existed.)

"I'll tell you! 'Here's to the land that gave me birth, here's to the flag she flies, here's to the dumdy-dum-dum-dum ——' "

And so on. Every one has a song he wants sung, and it seldom is the song that any one else wants, although "Heidelberg" and "Kiss Me Again" usually win out against the field because more people remember the tune and the words don't matter so much. "Kiss Me Again," in fact, can be, and usually is, carried through to the end with no other words than "Kiss Me Again" being used. The only drawback to this number is that it calls for quite a vocal range toward the end, resulting in all but two or three lusty singers dropping out in terror before the final rousing notes have been given their full value. Not quite enough people usually drop out, however.

I have never known it to fail that if only one man remembers the words to a certain song, he remembers all the words to all the verses and perhaps one or two

159

parodies which were considered very funny at the time. And there is some sort of fever which lays hold of any one who is in full possession of words to a song which renders him impervious to the glares and interruptions of the others and makes him plow doggedly ahead through the entire number, his eyes bulging with pride and the cords of his neck straining with the effort of demonstrating his ability. It is an irritating sight, unless it happens to be I who am remembering the words. Then it is inconceivable that the others should not be interested. Which they are not.

If organized community singing must be done (and evidently it must) the thing to do is divide the town up into quartets, preferably all male with no sopranos, and put each quartet down in a good smoky back room where the air is bad, and let nature take its course. I know of nothing more soothing or productive of good feeling than to get three other guys, one of whom is not really a natural bass but who will fake it if some one else will carry the baritone, and then to go into a huddle for an evening of ripe, rich swipes. With such little groups tearing off "Mandy Lee, I Love You" and "Way Down Yonder in the Cornfield" all over town, not much harm can come to the community, unless perhaps there should be a big blaze started in the town hall and some of the firemen should happen to be engaged in singing at the time. Then it would just be the town hall's hard luck, that's all.

In the meantime, don't forget: The Welsh national eisteddfod at Llanelly on Aug. 8. Let's make this just the best eisteddfod ever!

"Go Down, Sweet Jordan"

THERE used to be a time when four Negroes could get together and tear off a little ripe harmony and nobody thought anything of it except that it sounded great. Now, since spirituals have been taken up socially, you have got to know counterpoint and the "History of the Key of Four Flats" in order really to appreciate them.

What used to be just plain "Swing Low, Sweet Chariot" in the old brown book of college songs, along with "Seeing Nellie Home" and "Clementine," is now a manifestation of the growth of the Chariot Motif from the ancient African tap-dance through the muted eighth note into assonance and dissonance. And over your ears.

Having heard and read so much about the history of the Negro spiritual, I have been moved to look into the matter myself and have unearthed a large block of data which I am going to work into a book, to be called *The Legal Aspects of the Negro Spiritual*. It will take up the little-known origins of the spiritual in Africa and bring it right down to the present day, or rather to December 5, when the book will come out (and go in again after seeing its own shadow).

Commentators and experts on the spiritual do not seem to realize that this particular form of harmony comes from the old African "vegetable-humming," dating back to the early seventeenth century and perhaps later. "Vegetable-humming" or *blakawa* was a chant taken part in by certain members of the tribe who wished they were vegetables and who thought that by humming loudly enough (with the tenor carrying the air) the God of the Harvest would turn them into vegetables and they could get their wish. There is no case on record of any one of them ever having been turned into a vegetable, but they kept on humming just the same, and it is in this strange form of religious ecstasy that the spiritual as we know it had its origin.

Let us take, for example, the spiritual, "Roll Down Jordan, Roll Up de Lord." This is one of the best songs for our purpose, as it contains the particular harmonic combinations which are also found in the "vegetable-humming," that is, C, G-sharp, A, and E, sliding up very wickedly into D-flat, G-natural, B-flat, and E-sharp. In case the G-sharp slips a little too much and gets into H, the singer must open his mouth very wide but stop making sounds altogether.

The first verse to "Roll Down Jordan, Roll Up de Lord" goes:

"Roll down Jordan; roll up de Lord;
Roll down Jordan; roll up de Lord;
Roll down Jordan; roll up de Lord;
Roll down Jordan; roll up de Lord!"

We then find the whole spirit of the thing changing and the evangelical note so common among Africans creeping into the second verse:

"Roll down de Lord; roll up Jordan;
Roll down de Lord; roll up Jordan;

162

Roll down de Lord; roll up Jordan;
Roll down de Lord; roll up Jordan;
Hey-hey!"

Thus, you will see, does the modern chant derive from the old wheat-cake dance, which in its turn, derived from Chicago to Elkhart in four hours (baby talk). In this dance we seem to see the native women filing into the market-place in the early morning to offer up their prayer to the God of Corn on the Cob for better and more edible crops ("O God of the Harvest! Give us some corn that we can eat. That last was terrible! Amen"). The dance itself was taken part in by the local virgins and such young men of the tribe as were willing to be seen out with them. They marched once around the market-place beating drums until someone told them to shut up. Then they seated themselves in a semi-circle, facing inward, and rocked back and forth, back and forth. This made some of them sick and they had to be led out. The rest sat there rocking and crooning until they were eighteen years old, at which time they all got up and went home, pretty sore at themselves for having wasted so much time.

We have now seen how the old tribes handled the problem of what to sing and how to prevent people from singing it. The slave trade, bringing these Negroes and their descendants over to America, foisted the problem on the United States. For a long time, owing to the colored people not knowing that they were developing a national folk song, nothing was done about it. The Negroes just sat around on piece of corn-pone and tried out various kinds of swipes which they aggravated by the use of the banjo. One of the favorite songs of this era ran thus:

(*Basses*) M-m-m-m-m-m-m-m-m-m.
(*Tenors*) M-m-m-m-m-m-m-m-m-m.
(*First tenor solo*) M-m-m-m-m-m-m-m-m-m.
(*Second tenor solo*) M-m-m-m-m-m-m-m-m-m.
(*Unison*) Comin' fer to carry me home.

Under this ran the banjo accompaniment something like this:

> Plunky-plunky-plunky-plunky,
> Plunky-plunky-plunky-plunky,
> Plunky-plunky-plunky-plunky,
> Plunky-plunky-plunky-plunky,
> Plunk!

Here we find for the first time some evidence of the spirit of the whole race stirring in its captivity. We seem to see the women filing into the market-place in the early morning to raise their prayer to the God of the Harvest—I guess that goes with the other song.

Gradually, during the Reconstruction Period following the Civil War, carpetbaggers from the North came in and organized these singing groups into glee-clubs, each with a leader and white gloves. They taught the basses to sing "Zum-zum-zum-zum" instead of "M-m-m-m-m-m-m" and wrote extra verses to many of the numbers to be sung as encores. The colored people didn't know what to make of all this and many of them stopped singing entirely and went in for tap-dancing. But the popularization of the Negro spiritual was on its way and special writers were assigned to the job of making

164

up words which would sound rather native and yet would tell a story. It was found that only four words were needed for each song, as they were always repeated. Thus we have the growth of such songs as "Carryin' de Clouds on Jehovah's Back," "Ain't Gwine ter Pray fer de Old Black Roan," and "Ramona." The growth of the narrative in such songs can be traced in the following, entitled "All God's Fish is A-comin' Home":

> "Oh, I went fer ter see de lightnin',
> Oh, I went fer ter see de lightnin',
> Oh, I went fer ter see de lightnin',
>   But de lightnin' warn't ter home.

> "Oh, I went fer ter see de thunder,
> Oh, I went fer ter see de thunder,
> Oh, I went fer ter see de thunder,
>   But de thunder warn't ter home.

> "Oh, I went fer ter see de rain (pronounced
>   'ray-un'),
> Oh, I went fer ter see de rain,
> Oh, I went fer ter see de rain,
>   But de rain warn't ter home."

And so on the song goes, with the singer going to see, in rapid succession, the fog, the light mist, the snow, the oysters, the river, Lake Placid, the man about coming to carry away the ashes, and finally the Lord, none of them being at home except the Lord and he was busy.

This marks the final development of the spiritual as a regenerative force and also marks the point at which I give up. I would, however, like to hear four good colored singers again without having to put my glasses on to follow the libretto.

165

"One Minute, Please!"

I AM known as a bad business man from one end of the country to just a little beyond the same end. Practically every one in my class in kindergarten went into business after graduation, and when I say business I mean business. Whenever I see them now they are always dressed up in stiff shirts and are making marks on the backs of envelopes. Get me a hundred of my old schoolmates together and let them talk from 9 A.M. until almost dinner time and I won't understand a word they are saying. It is only around dinner time that I begin to catch a glimmer of sense and then they have to come right out and say "Martini" or "Green turtle soup." At this point I join the party.

But not until I have had it said to me eight or a dozen times that I ought to be more businesslike. "Good old Bob," they say (those of them who remember that my name is "Bob"), "you are just a sucker to be so impractical. Why don't you let us take some of your money and triple it for you?"

Leaving aside the question "What money?" I am frankly at a loss for something to say. Here I am, just a dreamer, and there they are, captains of industry, or, at any rate, second lieutenants. They have the advantage of me.

Of course, if I wanted to, I might point out that out of a possible $5000 which I have made since I left school I have had $3000 worth of good food (all of which has

166

gone into making bone and muscle and some nice fat),
$1500 worth of theatre tickets, and $500 worth of candy;
whereas many of my business friends have simply had
$5000 worth of whatever that stock was which got so
yellow along about last November.

I was sympathetic with all the boys at that time and
even advanced a little cash in a sparing manner, but I
couldn't help remembering the days during the summer
when I had to sit and listen to them say: "Well, I made
$650,000 over the week-end. What will you have, Bob,
old man?" And all the time I was, in my old impractical
way, sinking my money into silk neckties (which I still
have) and throwing it away on life-giving beefsteaks.

I do not intend to dwell on this phase of life's whirl-
igig, however. Who can tell, perhaps some day even we
spendthrifts may find ourselves short of cash. In the
meantime, those of us who have nothing but fripperies
to show for our money have had a good laugh. At least
we've got the fripperies.

What I do want to dwell on is the point that there
are still a great many practices which are considered
businesslike and efficient and which any one of us old
dreamers could improve upon and speed up. Now you
sit still and read this. I have sat still and listened to you
long enough.

First, there is the question of business telephoning.
During the last five or six years there has spread throughout the business world a method of telephoning which,
so far as I am concerned, bids fair to destroy all channels
of business communication. If it keeps up, I, for one,
will go back to the old Indian runner and carrier pigeon

167

methods. I won't stand for this another day. In fact, I stopped standing for it a year ago.

I refer to the delayed pass play, so popular among busy executives. In this play your busy executive, when he wants to get me on the telephone (why he should want to get me on the telephone is a mystery), says to his secretary: "Get me Mr. Benchley on the wire, Miss Whatney." You see, he hasn't got the time to get me himself, what with all those stocks he has to tend to; so he has Miss Whatney do it for him. So far, pretty good! Miss Whatney looks up my number in the book and gives it to the operator at the switchboard, thereby releasing the busy executive for other duties, such as biting off the end of a cigar or drawing circles on his scratch pad.

The scene now changes and we see me, the impractical dreamer, sitting at an old typewriter with nothing to do but finish an article which was due the day before. My telephone rings and I, in my slipshod, impractical way, answer it. And what do I get for my pains?

"Is this Vanderbilt 0647? Is Mr. Benchley there? Just a minute, please!"

Having nothing to do but wool-gather, I wait. In about two minutes I hear another female voice saying: "Is this Mr. Benchley? Just a minute, please, Mr. Kleek wants to speak to you."

Remember, it is Mr. Kleek who is calling *me* up. I don't want to speak to Mr. Kleek. I wouldn't care if I never spoke to him. In fact, I am not sure that I know who Mr. Kleek is.

"Just a minute, please," comes the voice again. "Mr. Kleek is talking on another wire."

168

Now, fascinating as this information is, it really wasn't worth getting up out of my chair for. Mr. Kleek could be busy on eight other wires and my life would go on just about the same. Am I to be called away from my work to be told that a Mr. Kleek is talking on another wire? I think this out as I stand there waiting.

Finally, after several minutes, I hear a man's voice.

"Hello," it says gruffly: "who is this?" I am not only to be told to wait until Mr. Kleek is ready to speak to me, but I am to be treated by Mr. Kleek as if I had infringed on his time. At this point I frankly flare up.

"Who is this yourself?" I snarl. "This was your idea, not mine!"

Then evidently Miss Whatney tells Mr. Kleek that she has got Mr. Benchley on the wire, and he is somewhat mollified. But I want to tell you, Mr. Kleek, that by that time I am not on the wire any longer and you can stick that telephone ear-piece into the side of your head. Furthermore, from now on, the minute I am called to the telephone and told to wait a minute, that Mr. Anybody wants to speak to me, I hang up so quickly that the hook drops off. If Mr. Kleek or any other busy executive wants to speak to me he can be there within four seconds after I answer or he can put in the call again. I may be just an old wool-gatherer, but I want to gather my wool somewhere else than at a telephone receiver.

It is possible that the telephone has been responsible for more business inefficiency than any other agency except laudanum. It has such an air of pseudo-efficiency about it that people feel efficient the minute they take the receiver off the hook. A business man could be talk-

169

ing with Ajax, the mechanical chess player, on the other end of the wire and still feel he was getting somewhere, simply because to any one passing the door he looks as if he were very busy. There is something about saying "O. K." and hanging up the receiver with a bang that kids a man into feeling that he has just pulled off a big deal, even if he has only called up Central to find out the correct time. For this reason business men use the telephone exclusively when almost any other form of communication would be quicker.

In the old days when you wanted to get in touch with a man you wrote a note, sprinkled it with sand, and gave it to a man on horseback. It probably was delivered within half an hour, depending on how big a lunch the horse had had. But in these busy days of rush-rush-rush, it sometimes is a week before you can catch your man on the telephone. The call is put in, but he is out. You tell your secretary to keep calling, but, if the man takes any kind of care of himself at all, he is out most all day in the fresh air. So day after day the secretary keeps calling and, in this way, autumn turns into winter and winter to spring. Perhaps you never get him.

A busy executive said to me the other day in an exasperated tone: "Aren't you ever in? I have been trying to get you on the telephone for five days. What do you do with your time, cut lawns?" You see, I am the one who was in the wrong. I was the impractical one.

I might have told him about that new invention called the "typewriter," whereby, if you can't get a man on the telephone, you can drop him a note which will reach him the next morning. Or I also might have told him that I was in my office all the time, but was so busy

working that I had left word with the telephone operator not to bother me with time-wasting calls from business men. In either case, dropping me a note would have
saved him four days of telephoning. But apparently note-
dropping is considered a relic of Civil War days and is
not to be considered in the bustle of modern business.
You must use the telephone, even if it doesn't get you
anywhere.

The telephone is the particular pet of the go-getter
who won't take no for an answer. He has a passion for
long-distance calls. Let us say that his organization is
getting up a dinner in Chicago and wants to get an
after-dinner speaker from New York. The go-getter is,
of course, chairman of the dinner committee because
he gets things done. He guarantees to get the New York
speaker. "Leave it to me," he says, knowingly. And, even
as he says it, he is putting in a long-distance call for New
York. Bingo—like that! The New York man answers
and gets the following:

"This is Ferley of the Autumn Coat and Suit speaking! We're holding a dinner here on Feb. 10, and you're
coming out to speak for us!—O, yes, you are! I won't
take 'no' for an answer. . . . O, yes, you can—I'll call
those people up and tell them you're coming to us. . . .
Now, not another word!—See you on the 10th!"

With this he hangs up and reports to the committee
that he has the speaker sewed up. The fact that the New
York man can't go to Chicago on the 10th and has no
intention of going doesn't enter into the calculations at
all. No one is supposed to be able to resist the man with
the telephone personality. He sweeps everything before
him.

The only drawback is that, two days before the dinner, when it is found out that the New York speaker meant what he said and really isn't coming, the go-getter has to go-get somebody through a local agency to do card tricks for the diners. "That's the trouble with dealing with these literary guys," he thunders. "You can't count on them!" And he puts in another long-distance call just to quiet his nerves.

And so it goes through life. There are the doers and the dreamers, the men who make every second count and the men who waste their time with nothing to show for it. The first are the business men of the country, the others are the impractical fellows who write and draw pictures. Or perhaps it is just the other way 'round. I always get these things mixed.

The Mystery of Bridge-Building

I AM not much of a one to be writing on bridge building, having never really built a bridge myself, but if the reader (you) will overlook a little vagueness in some of the directions, I myself will overlook the fact that the reader has no right to criticize, unless, of course, he happens to be a professional bridge builder himself.

It has always seemed to me that the most difficult part of building a bridge would be the start. What does a man do first when he sets out to build a bridge? Granted he has his plans all drawn up and enough food and drink to last him a month. He is standing on one bank of a river and wants to build a bridge across to the other bank. What is the first thing that he does? (I seem to be asking all the questions.)

I suppose that he takes a shovel and digs a little hole, and has his picture taken doing it. Maybe somebody waves a flag. I have seen photographs of such a ceremony, but they never show what happens next. Frankly, I would be up against it if any one were to put me on one bank of a river and say: "Build a bridge across to the other bank." I might be able to finish it if some one would start it for me, but as for making the first move I would be left blushing furiously.

I once heard of a man who was confronted by just this emergency. It had got around somehow that he was an authority on bridgework (as a matter of fact, he was a dentist), and when the people in a neighboring town wanted a bridge built they sent for him. He was an easy-going sort of chap, and after they had given him a big dinner and a good cigar he didn't have the heart to tell them that he really knew nothing about the sort of bridge building that they wanted. He kept meaning to tell them, but they were so nice and evidently had so much confidence in him that he hated to spoil their good time, especially after he had eaten their dinner. So he just sat tight and let things take their course.

Pretty soon he found himself on the left bank of the river, with a brass band huddled around him and a lot of people in frock coats, and after some one had read Lincoln's Gettysburg address he was given a gold shovel and told to go ahead. Fortunately the people didn't stick around and watch him, as they figured out that he might be embarrassed by so many spectators, so he stuck the shovel in the ground and waved good-by to every one, and then bent over as if he were going to work. As a matter of fact, he was in a terrible state of mind.

He looked across at the other bank and tried to figure out how far it was. Then he looked behind him and tried to figure out how far that was. He thought that maybe the thing to do was to go and get the bridge made somewhere else, bring it to this spot, and stick one end of it in the hole he had dug and then swing it around until the other end was over the other bank, but that didn't seem practical. So he sat down and began writing some letters he had been meaning to write for months. Then he started throwing shovels full of dirt into the river, hoping against hope that he might get enough of it piled up on the river bottom to make a kind of bridge in itself, but he couldn't even make it show above the surface in one spot.

Just then a man with a rod and a fish basket happened to stroll by and asked him what he was doing.

"You will just laugh when I tell you," said the bridge builder.

"No, I won't, honestly," said the fisherman.

"Then you don't laugh easily," said the bridge builder. "I'm building a bridge."

"And a very smart thing to be doing, too," replied the fisherman. "One never can have too many bridges." Then he added, "You see, I didn't laugh."

This so endeared him to the bridge builder that he offered the stranger a drink, and one thing led to another until they both were sitting on the river bank talking about old songs they used to sing when they were boys.

"Do you remember one that used to go, "Hello ma baby, hello ma lady, hello ma ragtime gal'?" asked one.

" 'Send me a kiss by wire, honey, ma heart's on fire'?" added the other. "Is that the one you mean?"

"It sure is," said the other. "And then it went, 'If you refuse me, honey, you lose me, then I'll be left alone.' "

" 'So, baby, telephone and tell me I'se your own,' " they both sang in unison.

Well, this sort of thing went on for months and months, until they had exhausted all the old songs they used to know and got to making up new ones. The bridge expert forgot entirely what he was there for and the fisherman had never really known, so he had nothing to forget. People used to come over from the town to see how the bridge was coming on and then would tiptoe away again when they saw the two having such a good time. Finally they got some one else to build the bridge, starting from the other side of the river, and what was the surprise of the original bridge expert one day to look up from his game of cribbage with the fisherman and find that they were directly in the way of the vehicular traffic from a brand new bridge. You may be sure that he joined in the laughter, even though the joke was in a way on him. But he saw the fun of the thing, and that is better than any bridge building. What we need in this world is fewer bridges and more fun.

However, the problem of the bridge expert which has just been cited doesn't do much to help those of us who don't understand how a bridge is built. What we want to know is how the second man that the town got went about the job. He evidently knew something about it, for he got the thing done.

I think that it is all that stuff in the air over the river that puzzles me. I can understand the things they build on the banks all right. You go about building those just as you would go about building a house, except, of course, for the windows and front porch. But all those wires and hangings which are suspended from apparently nowhere and yet are strong enough to hold up any number of automobiles and trolley cars that take it into their heads to cross the river. There is something very fishy about those. Who supports them? I don't like the looks of it, frankly.

Of course, I suppose that if I had gone a little further in mathematics in school I would be a little easier in my mind about bridges. There is evidently something beyond plane geometry which I don't know about and which may hold the key to this mystery. Maybe it's in plane geometry. I missed a couple of days when I had a sore throat, and perhaps those are the days when the geometry class took up bridge building. Or it is quite possible that I actually studied it and didn't absorb it. I would say that my absorption point in mathematics was about .007, and I would not be surprised to find out that I had missed the whole point entirely.

However, even though your engineer has it all worked out mathematically on paper, with figures and digits all over the place, I still don't see how they get those wires up there in the air or how the wires are induced to hold things up. I studied physics and I'm no fool. You can't tell me that all that weight isn't pulling down, and my question is, "Down from what?"

I don't mean to be nasty about this thing, or narrow-minded. Neither do I incline to the theory of witch-craft—much. There is a man in India, so they tell me, who throws a rope up in the air and then climbs up it, which is evidently the principle of bridge building. But that man in India is supposed to be a fakir, and, according to some theories, the spectators are hypnotized into thinking they see him climb the rope, whereas he is actually not doing it at all. This would be a good explanation of bridges if it were not for the fact that you can't hypnotize a truck into thinking it is crossing a river.

Of course, the old-fashioned covered bridge is easy enough to understand. People could wade right out into those rivers and stick the posts in by hand, or at any rate could get planks long enough to reach across. All that was necessary was to get good planks that would rumble. And, by the way, what has become of the old-fashioned rumbling plank? You never hear planks rumbling today as they used to on those old covered bridges. I once spent the night in a farmhouse which I later found out was near a covered bridge. In the middle of the night I heard what I thought was thunder; so I got up and shut the window. The room got very hot in about half an hour, so, hearing no more thunder, I thought that the storm had passed us by, and got up and opened the window again. In about ten minutes there was another rumble; this time very loud. With a bound I was out of bed and had the window down in a jiffy. Then came half an hour of stifling again, with a pronounced odor of burning hay from the mattress. I got up and looked out the window. The stars were shining. So up she came again and I went back to bed after stepping on both my shoes, which were lying upside down by the bed. This went on at intervals of half an hour all night, until I finally overcame my fear of thunderstorms and decided to let the lightning come right in and get into bed with me if it wanted to, rather than shut the window again. I have already given away the point of this story, so I need hardly say that I found out in the morning that it actually had been thunder that I had heard and that the town on the other side of the mountain had had a bad storm all night. The covered bridge, however, could have been responsible for the rumbling if it had wanted to.

This little anecdote, exciting and amusing as it has been for all of us, I am sure, has drawn us quite a long way from the theme of this treatise, which, you will remember, was, "What Sort of Trickery Goes Into the Building of Bridges?" I don't happen to know many bridge engineers, so I am unable to say whether they are tricksters as a class. In fact, the only one that I know built a privately owned toll bridge across a river once, and then found that the township ran a free bridge about half a mile down the river around a bend which he hadn't seen before. Se he hung his bridge with Japanese lanterns and limited it to rickshas and spent his vacations fishing from it.

But, aside from possibly taking on a job for building a pontoon bridge, which I could do if I had enough boats, I am distinctly not in the market for a bridge contract until some one explains the principle of the thing more clearly to me.

I once read of a man who was caught in a hotel fire and broke open one of those glass cases containing what is known as a "fire ax." Then, as he stood there, ax in hand, watching little curls of smoke coming up through the floor, he tried to figure out what to do with the ax. He could chop a hole in the floor and let more fire up, or he could chop a hole in the wall and make a nice draft. Aside from those two courses of action he seemed to be saddled with an ax and that was all. After waving it weakly around his head once or twice, thinking maybe to frighten the fire away, he just stood there, making imaginary chopping motions, until the firemen came and carried him out still asking, "What do I do with this?"

Such will be my dilemma when some one puts a shovel in my hand and says: "How about building a bridge?"

"They're off!"

THERE are several spectacular ways in which I could dissipate a fortune, if I were to have one left to me, but one of them is not horse-racing.

Some day you may read of my daredevil escapades with a team of arch-duchesses on the Riviera in which "Mad Bob" (that will be I) rides up and down the Promenade des Anglais on a high-powered car's running-board throwing out burning mille-franc notes at the people (all of whom love me for my wild, likeable eccentricities). You may read of someone who has discovered me, a grey-haired, distinguished-looking old derelict, pacing the water-front of Port Said, living on the pittance furnished me by friends whom I had wined and dined in the old days when I was known as "The Playboy of Two Continents," before a group of international bankers conspired against me to wipe out my entire fortune at one *coup*. (I hate those bankers already, just thinking about it). But you will never hear about my taking my life at a race-course—unless it is from sheer confusion. That is one thing you don't have to worry about, in case you worry about me at all.

Fond as I am of horses when meeting them personally (and give me a handful of sugar and I will make friends with any horse—or lose my hand up to the wrist in the attempt) I am strangely unmoved when I see them rac-

ing each other up and down a track. A great calm descends on me at the cry "They're Off!" and, as the race proceeds, this calm increases in intensity until it is practically a coma, from which I have to be aroused by friends telling me which horse won.

Much of this coolness towards horse-racing is due to the fact that I almost never have any money up. I have no scruples in the matter (except that old New England scruple against losing money), but I never seem to be able to get the hang of just how the betting is done. By the time I have decided what horse I would like to bet on, everybody seems to have disappeared, either through indifference to my betting plans or because the race is on. I hear other people betting, but I never can quite see whom they are betting with. The whole thing is more or less chaotic to me.

In the second place, I never can *see* a horse-race. Of course, when you go to a race in England, like the Grand National, you don't expect to see. All you do is listen very carefully and peer into the mist and, when you hear the crowd murmur "They're Off!" go around back to a refreshment tent and munch on a cold meat-pie until you think it is time for the race to be finished. Then go to the door of the tent and someone (who didn't see the finish either) will tell you who won. That is the Sport of Kings as England knows it.

In this country, you usually can see the course, but I personally have a great deal of trouble in finding out where the horses are. Part of this is due to my inability to manipulate long-range glasses. I can swing them jauntily by my side before the race starts, and I can hold them up to my eyes (until my arms get tired—then to hell with them) but I can't seem to see anything except an indistinct blur of grass and an object which later turns out to be the back of the head of one of the officials. Even if I find the horses when they are grouped at the barrier, I lose them the minute they start out and spend my time sweeping the horizon for them while my friends are muttering "Look at that! Look at him come up! There goes Captain's Garter! Here comes Onion Soup!" The last time I used field glasses at a horse race I thought I saw a rowboat in the distance manned by a suspiciously large number of oarsmen; so I haven't felt

182

like using the glasses since then. With my naked eye I can at least see the surrounding country, and without the complication of strange rowboats.

I have therefore given up the use of glasses entirely and carry them just for looks. (I am even thinking of giving that up, too, as I have been told that they don't *look* right on me.) With the naked eye at least I can see the grass clearly and, at Belmont Park, there are some very pretty fountains to watch in case the race itself has eluded you. Even with my eyes free to roam as they will, I lose the horses before they have gone a hundred yards. Everyone else seems to know where they are, even people with much worse eyesight than mine (and I may say that my eyesight is very good as a general thing), but the whole affair becomes a mystery to me until suddenly I find that they are at the last turn and into the homestretch. Then comes the problem of finding out which horse is which.

It is, I will admit, a very pretty sight to see a lot of horses coming in at the finish, but it would be much more exciting for me if I could distinguish the various colors. Insofar as I have any favorites at all, they are always the horses who carry a bright red, because that is the only color that means anything to me at the finish. These yellow and pink mixtures get all confused with the baby-blues and blood-oranges when they get bunched together, and I am constantly upset by the spectacle of what seems to me to be two jockeys on one horse. I don't like to admit after the finish that I haven't been able to detect the winner, and so a great many times I am completely in the dark unless I overhear a chance remark or see an early edition of the papers.

This makes going to the races something of a mockery.

Then, too, there is another source of confusion for me in the varying lengths of the races they see fit to run. I think that I am correct in saying that one has a right to expect that any race shall finish down in front of the grandstands. I don't mean to be arbitrary about this, but that is the way it seems to me. All right, then. The last race I saw at Belmont Park (New York) began where they all begin—that is, just beyond my range of vision, over at the right. The horses, as near as I could tell, ran straight away along the other side of the course, meaning nothing as far as I was concerned. Then, just as they reached the far turn, they seemed to give the whole thing up as a bad job and began running in different directions. I though that maybe it was a game like hare-and-hounds, that one bunch of horses went North and another went South and still others East and West, with the ones who got back on to the course first, winning. But no. It seems that the race was over, 'way out there, and they were simply dispersing for the afternoon. In other words, nobody in the stands (unless they happened to know black art and were able to work long-range glasses) had any idea as to which horse won. I was particularly fortunate in not caring.

But, aside from the strain of trying to keep the horses within your range of vision and telling which is which, there is another feature of horse-racing which seems to me a little irksome. That is the intervals between races. If left to myself I would be inclined to read a good book between times, or even during the races themselves. But this, evidently, is not allowed. You must get up as soon as a race is over and go out behind the stands and walk around in the paddock. Just what good this is supposed to do I never could figure out. You look at the horses and you look at the jockeys and you say "How are you?" to a lot of people who are walking around looking at the horses and the jockeys. But as for changing anything at that late hour, even your mind on a bet, the whole thing seems a little futile. Most of the people who walk around in the paddock just before a race don't know whether a horse looks good or not. They just look. They make marks with a pencil and try to appear "in the

know" (*slang phrase*), but even *I* know that they aren't getting anywhere by doing it. Unless a horse in the paddock is obviously walking on three legs, or a jockey is obviously cockeyed, this walking around is just walking around and I can just walk around at home or in Times Square. I don't have to go out to a race-course to do it.

Personally, I always get lost when I walk around in the paddock. I start out with, let us say, three friends, whose company is sufficiently pleasing to me to make me leave my comfortable subway or corner drug-store and go out to the track in the first place. We amble around under the trees for a few minutes, look at a couple of horses who would much rather not be looked at, and then, all of a sudden, I am alone. My friends have diappeared into comparatively thin air. I turn to the right and run into a horse. I turn to the left and run into several people who might as well be horses as far as anything in common we have together. Then I get a little panicky. I begin rushing. I try to find the clubhouse. It, too, has disappeared. There are a lot of people about, but I don't seem to know any of them. Once in a while I recognize a man I know who works in the box office of a theatre, but he always looks so worried that I dare not speak to him. I feel that maybe I am out of place. Later I find that I am. The hot sun beats down on me and I get to crying. The whole thing takes on the aspect of a bad dream. Even if I do get back to the stands, I merely am getting back to further confusion. There really is nothing left for me to do but go home. And I don't know how to get home. (*I am writing this out by the paddock at the last race-course I went to. Will someone who reads this, and who lives near Saratoga, come and get me out?*)

Bringing Back the Morris Dance

I DON'T know why I never thought to speak of it before, but we don't do nearly enough Morris-dancing in this country. These fine early summer days (or early winter days, or whenever you read this) it seems a shame to be devoting ourselves to golf and tennis and drinking when we might be out of doors prancing around a pole and falling down every few feet.

In Merrie Englandie they used to have quite a good time doing this, and there is no reason why we shouldn't today, except that good poles are hard to get. Poles with ribands on them are practically unknown. The thing to do is get a pole and put the ribands on yourself, and then you are sure that they are fresh.

Of course, it is not necessary to have a pole for your Morris dance, but it is better because then you have something to lean against when you get tired. (I am tired before I start, just thinking about it.) The chief thing for Morris-dancing is a smock and lots of ribands.

I am sorry to keep harping on this riband business, but you are just nobody in Morris-dancing circles unless you have a lot of ribands hanging off you. These serve to float in the wind and to trip you up. I am going right ahead in this thesis on the assumption that "ribands" are the same as our "ribbons," although I haven't looked it up. If they are something entirely different, then I am getting myself into a terrible mix-up and might better stop right here.

Bells are also worn strapped to the dancers' legs to give warning to the other dancers and show where each individual is at any given time. These dances used to run on 'way into the night sometimes, and without the bells there would be nasty collisions and perhaps serious injury. It is essential that the bells be strapped tightly to the legs, otherwise the dancer will have to keep stooping and hitching them up every few steps, thereby spoiling the symmetry of the dance figure. If the bells *are* loose and there is no way of tightening them, the next best thing is to have a very small child run along beside the dancer and hold them up. It would have to be a *very* small child, though, so small as to be almost repulsive.

I had always thought (when I thought of it at all) that the name "Morris dance" came from William Morris who designed the old Morris chairs. By the way, did you ever see a Morris chair that *wasn't* old? They must have been new *some*time, when they were bought, but by the time anyone ever got to looking at them the seats were all sunken in and the arms covered with cigarette burns. Perhaps that was the way William Morris designed them. I frankly don't know. As I look back on them now, it also seems that they were always awfully low, so low as to be almost a part of the floor. It was always very difficult to get up out of one, once you got in, and I wouldn't be surprised if a great many people are still sitting in them, which would account for a great many people that have been missing for a long time. Expeditions might be started to go and get missing people out of Morris chairs—or maybe you don't care.

Well, anyway, it *wasn't* that William Morris who worked up the Morris dance, because he came a great deal later and was too busy with chairs, anyway. I understand that the Moors in Spain did the first Morris dances, and called it the "Morisco," probably a trade name like "Nabisco" and "Delco." It is barely possible that one of the Marx Brothers' ancestors, named Mawruss, invented it and began that pleasing trick of nomenclature which has resulted in "Groucho," "Harpo," "Chico," and "Zeppo" among his descendants. At any rate, the dance that the Moors used to do was the "Morisco" and "Morris" was as near as the English could get the name. You would think that a great big nation like England could get the little name "Morisco" right. But no.

We are told that, in Merrie Englandie, one of the dancers was always decked out as Robin Hood "with a magpye's plume to his capp and a russat bearde," which is as lousy spelling as you will see grouped together in any one sentence anywhere. At first, the only music was that of the bells, but that got pretty tiresome after a while and they brought out a flute, or "tabor," which probably added nothing. I can, offhand, think of nothing more dismal.

Of course, I hope that you don't think that I am under the impression that the Morris dance was the *first* outdoor dancing done by people. I am not quite *that* much of a ninny. The first records that we have of such things are those of the Egyptians about 5000 B.C. (And what a long time ago *that* was!) Nobody knows what they had to dance about in 5000 B.C., but they were hard at it, for we find pictures of them dancing on their sarcophagi. That is, they didn't dance on their sarcophagi, but they drew pictures on their sarcophagi, of dancing, which must have been almost as painful. In this dance, eight maidens from the local maidenry danced around and around with no particular idea in mind, finally falling down when they got tired, which was in anywhere from ten to fifteen minutes. This left them with the rest of the afternoon free, but they probably weren't good for much.

Most of all folk dancing that followed this has been based on the same idea—round, and round, and round, and then stop. In the Chinese dances they did a great deal of banging as they danced, striking swords on shields and scowling, but there is no record of anyone ever getting hurt. They got awfully tired, though. That seems to be the story of all group dancing through the ages, people getting awfully tired. It is a wonder that no one ever thought of just not dancing at all.

Sometimes, of course, the dances did mean something, usually an appeal to the Rain God to do something about the crops. The Egyptians had a dance like this, but one year they did it *too* well and got nothing *but* rain; so they had to work in a figure which was an appeal to the Sun God to come and drive away the Rain God. This resulted in a lot of hard feeling between the Sun God and the Rain God and the entire dance had to be discontinued, with the result that, for about fifty years, no crops came up at all.

But we are getting away from our Morris dance, which is perhaps just as well. By the sixteenth century you would have thought that people would be working up something new in the line of dancing, but the only difference between the Morris dance and that one of the Egyptians was the bells on the legs. The Egyptians also danced sideways a lot, which made it difficult for them to get anywhere much. The English rustics did know enough to dance forward and back, but that isn't much of a development for over six thousand years, is it?

A lot of people try to read a sex meaning into dancing, but that seems to me to be pretty far-fetched. By the time you have been panting and blowing around in a circle for five or ten minutes, keeping your mind steadily on maintaining your balance and not tripping, sex is about the *last* thing that would enter your head.

191

Havelock Ellis even goes so far as to say that all life is essentially a dance, that we live in a rhythm which is nothing but a more cosmic form of dancing. This may be true of some people, but there are others, among whom I am proud to count myself, to whom life is static, even lethargic, and who are disciples of the Morris who designed the Morris chair rather than the Morris of the dance.

Havelock Ellis can dance through life if he wants to, but I think I'll sit this one out, if you don't mind.

The Treasurer's Report

Author's Note

ABOUT eight years ago (eight, to be exact) I was made a member of a committee to plan a little Sunday night entertainment for some newspapermen who wanted to act. The committee was supposed to meet at a certain time, each member with some suggestions for sketches or song-numbers. (In order to get out of this morass of pussy-footing which I have got myself into, I will come right out and say that the "certain time" at which the committee was to meet was 8 P. M. on Sunday night.) At 7:15 P. M. I suddenly realized that I had no suggestions to offer for the entertainment.

As all the other members of the committee were conscientious workers, I felt considerably abashed. But as they were also charming and indulgent fellows, I knew that they would take my dereliction in good part if I could only take their minds off the business of the meeting and possibly put them in good humor with a comical story or a card-trick. So, on the way up in the taxi, I decided to make believe, when they called on me for my contribution, that I had misunderstood the purpose of the committee-meeting and had come prepared to account for the year's expenditures. These I jotted down on the back of an old shirt.

As is always the case with such elaborate trickery, my plan to escape censure by diverting the minds of the committee fell flat. They listened to my temporizing report and voted me a droll chap, but then they said: "And now what are your suggestions for the entertainment?" As I had to confess that I had none, it was agreed that, *faute de mieux,* I should elaborate the report I had just offered and perhaps acquire some skill in its delivery, and give that as my share of the Sunday night entertainment. At this moment my entire life changed its course.

I guess that no one ever got so sick of a thing as I, and all my friends, have grown of this Treasurer's Report. I did it every night and two matinees a week for nine months in the Third Music Box Revue. Following that, I did it for ten weeks in vaudeville around the country, I did it at banquets and teas, at friends' houses and in my own house, and finally went to Hollywood and made a talking movie of it. In fact, I have inflicted it on the public in every conceivable way except over the radio and dropping it from airplanes. But I have never written it. I have been able to throw myself into a sort of trance while delivering it, so that the horrible monotony of the thing made no impression on my nerve cells, but to sit down and put the threadbare words on paper has always seemed just a little too much to bear.

I am writing it out now more as a release than anything else. Perhaps, in accordance with Freudian theories, if I rid myself of this thing which has been skulking in the back of my mind for eight years, I shall be a normal man again. No one has to read it. I hope that no one does, for it doesn't read at all well. All I want to do is get it on paper and out of the way. I feel better already, just from having told all this. And please let's never bring the matter up again.

*　　*　　*

The report is delivered by an Assistant Treasurer who has been called in to pinch-hit for the regular Treasurer who is ill. He is not a very good public-speaker, this assistant, but after a few minutes of confusion is caught up by the spell of his own oratory and is hard to stop.

I shall take but a very few moments of your time this evening, for I realize that you would much rather be listening to this interesting entertainment than to a dry financial statement . . . but I *am* reminded of a story —which you have probably all of you heard.

It seems that there were these two Irishmen walking down the street when they came to a—oh, I should have said in the first place that the parrot which was hanging out in *front* of the store—or rather belonging to one of these two fellows—the *first* Irishman, that is—was— well, *any*way, this parrot——

(After a slight cogitation, he realizes that, for all practical purposes, the story is as good as lost; so he abandons it entirely and, stepping forward, drops his facile, story-telling manner and assumes a quite spurious businesslike air.)

Now, in connection with reading this report, there are one or two points which Dr. Murnie wanted brought up in connection with it, and he has asked me to bring them up in connec—to bring them up.

In the first place, there is the question of the work which we are trying to do up there at our little place at Silver Lake, a work which we feel not only fills a very definite need in the community but also fills a very definite need—er—in the community. I don't think that many members of the Society realize just how big the work is that we are trying to do up there. For instance, I don't think that it is generally known that most of our boys are between the age of fourteen. We feel that, by taking the boy at this age, we can get closer to his real nature—for a boy *has* a very real nature, you may be sure—and bring him into closer touch not only with the school, the parents, and with each other, but also with the town in which they live, the country to whose flag they pay allegiance, and to the—ah— (*trailing off*) town in which they live.

Now the fourth point which Dr. Murnie wanted brought up was that in connection with the installation of the new furnace last Fall. There seems to have been considerable talk going around about this not having been done quite as economically as it might—have—been—done, when, as a matter of fact, the whole thing *was* done just as economically as possible—in fact, even *more* so. I have here a report of the Furnace Committee, showing just how the whole thing was handled from start to finish.

(*Reads from report, with considerable initial difficulty with the stiff covers.*)

Bids were submitted by the following firms of furnace contractors, with a clause stating that if we did not engage a firm to do the work for us we should pay them nothing for submitting the bids. This clause alone saved us a great deal of money.

The following firms, then, submitted bids:

Merkle, Wybigant Co., the Eureka Dust Bin and Shaker Co., The Elite Furnace Shop, and Harris, Birnbauer and Harris. The bid of Merkle, Wybigant being the lowest, Harris Birnbauer were selected to do the job.

(*Here a page is evidently missing from the report, and a hurried search is carried on through all the pages, without result.*)

Well, that pretty well clears up that end of the work. Those of you who contributed so generously last year to the floating hospital have probably wondered what became of the money. I was speaking on this subject only last week at our up-town branch, and, after the meeting, a dear little old lady, dressed all in lavender, came up on the platform, and, laying her hand on my arm, said: "Mr. So-and-So (calling me by name) Mr. So-and-So, what the hell did you do with all the money we gave you last year?" Well, I just laughed and pushed her off the platform, but it has occurred to the committee that perhaps some of you, like that little old lady, would be interested in knowing the disposition of the funds.

Now, Mr. Rossiter, unfortunately our treasurer—or rather Mr. Rossiter our *treasurer, unfortunately* is confined at his home tonight with a bad head-cold and I have been asked (*he hears someone whispering at him from the wings, but decides to ignore it*) and I have been asked if I would (*the whisperer will not be denied, so he goes over to the entrance and receives a brief message, returning beaming and laughing to himself*). Well, the joke seems to be on *me*! Mr. Rossiter has *pneumonia*!

Following, then, is a summary of the Treasurer's Report:

(Reads, in a very businesslike manner.)

During the year 1929—and by that is meant 1928—the Choral Society received the following in donations:

B. L. G.	$500
G. K. M.	500
Lottie and Nellie W.——	500
In memory of a happy summer at Rye Beach	10
Proceeds of a sale of coats and hats left in the boat-house	14.55
And then the Junior League gave a performance of "Pinafore" for the benefit of the Fund, which, unfortunately, resulted in a deficit of	$300
Then, from dues and charges	2,354.75
And, following the installation of the new furnace, a saving in coal amounting to $374.75—which made Dr. Murnie very happy, you may be sure.	
Making a total of receipts amounting to....	$3,645.75

This is all, of course, reckoned as of June.

In the matter of expenditures, the Club has not been so fortunate. There was the unsettled condition of business, and the late Spring, to contend with, resulting in the following—er—rather discouraging figures, I am afraid.

Expenditures	$23,574.85
Then there was a loss, owing to—several things—of	3,326.70

Car-fare . . . . $ 4,452.25

And then, Mrs. Rawlins' expense account,
  when she went down to see the work they
  are doing in Baltimore, came to $256.50,
  but I am sure that you will all agree that
  it was worth it to find out—er—what they
  are doing in Baltimore.

And then, under the general head of Odds
  and Ends 2,537.50

Making a total disbursement of (hur-
  riedly) $416,546.75

or a net deficit of—ah—several thousand dollars.

Now, these figures bring us down only to October.
In October my sister was married, and the house was all
torn up, and in the general confusion we lost track of
the figures for May and August. All those wishing the
approximate figures for May and August, however, may
obtain them from me in the vestry after the dinner,
where I will be with pledge cards for those of you who
wish to subscribe over and above your annual dues,
and I hope that each and every one of you here tonight
will look deep into his heart and (*archly*) into his
pocketbook, and see if he can not find it there to help
us to put this thing over with a bang (*accompanied by
a wholly ineffectual gesture representing a bang*) and
to help and make this just the biggest and best year the
Armenians have ever had . . . . . I thank you.

(*Exits, bumping into proscenium*)

The Homelike Hotel

ONE of the chief factors in the impending crash of the American Home as an institution is the present craze for making so many other places "homelike." We have homelike hotels, homelike barber shops, homelike auditoriums, and, so they tell me, homelike jails. A man can't go into a shop to get his skates sharpened without being made to feel that, if he has any appreciation for atmosphere at all, he ought really to send for his trunks and settle down and live right there in the skate-sharpening place. It is getting so that a home-loving man doesn't know which way to turn.

The hotels were the leaders in this campaign to make the home seem unhomelike by comparison. There was a time when a hotel was simply a place in which you slept; that is, if you were a good sleeper. You went in and registered and the man who pushed the book out at you turned his collar around and became the boy who took your bag up (possibly in one of those new-fangled lifts which you were sure would never replace the horse —at least, not in your affections).

The room, as you entered it, seemed to be a species of closet, smelling strongly of straw matting and rug threads, and, after a good look at the cherry bureau and its duplicating mirror and a tug at the rope which was coiled by the window in case you wanted to lasso any one, you turned out the hanging bulb over the bed (making a barely perceptible difference in the lighting of the room), and went out into the street to find a place to sit until bedtime. You would no more have thought of sitting in your room than you would have thought of getting into one of the bureau drawers and lolling around with a good book.

The first sign that the hotels were going in for the homey stuff in a big way was when they began hanging pictures on the walls. Either they didn't get the right pictures or they weren't hung properly. At any rate, the first hotel wall pictures were not successful in giving a homelike atmosphere. There were usually pastels showing two ladies with a fan, or two fans and one lady, with a man in knee breeches hovering about in the background. The girl with the broken jug was also a great favorite in the early days of hotel decoration. She still is doing very well, as a matter of fact, and you will find her in even the most up-to-date hostelries, giving what is hoped will be a final touch of bonhomie to the room. Well, she doesn't, and the sooner hotel managements are brought to realize it, the better it will be for them.

In fact, the whole problem of what pictures to hang on the walls of a hotel room is still in a state of flux. Until they get away from those little French garden scenes, with fans and sun dials as the chief props, they are never going to make me feel at home. And they do not help matters any by introducing etchings showing three boats lying alongside a dock or 17 geese flying South. It seems to me that the picture-hangers in hotels are striving too hard for good taste. What we want is not good taste in our hotel pictures, but something to look at. If you are going to live in the room with a picture all the rest of your life, good taste is all right. But for overnight give me something a little daring, with a lot of red in it.

There is another development in the equipment of hotel rooms which, while it does not exactly make the quarters attractive, keeps the guest interested while he is in the room. I refer to the quantity of reading matter which is placed at his disposal. This does not mean the little magazines that some hotels place by the bedside, in the hope that you will sit up so late reading that you will have to send down for a glass of milk and some crackers at midnight. I don't think people read those as much as they are supposed to. I don't think they even look at the pictures as much as they are supposed to.

But there is a trait which is almost universal among hotel guests and which is being catered to more and more by the managements. It is the tendency, amounting almost to a fascination, to read every word of every sign which is displayed around the room. You know very well that the chances are that not one sign out of ten will have any bearing on you or your life in that room. And yet, almost as soon as the bellboy has left, you amble around the room, reading little notices which have been slipped under the glass bureau top, tacked to the door, or tucked in the mirror. Not only do you read them once, but you usually go over them a second time, hoping that maybe there is something of interest which eluded you in the first reading.

I had occasion last week to share a hotel room with a man who was at Atlantic City with me on business. We were shown up by the boy, who went through all the regulation manoeuvres of opening the window (which

202

We spent the rest of the afternoon reading signs to our hearts' content

has to be shut immediately after he has gone), putting the bags on the stool (from which they have to be removed for unpacking), pushing open the door to the bathroom to show you where it is and to prevent your going into the next room by mistake, and making such financial adjustments as may be necessary. This completed, I reminded George that we were already late for our first appointment, and started for the door to go downstairs.

George, however, was busy at something over by the bureau. "Just a minute," he said, in a preoccupied tone. He was bending over the glass top as if he had found a deposit of something that might possibly turn out to be gold.

Impatiently I went over to grab him by the arm and pull him along. I saw he was reading a little notice, printed in red, which had been tucked under the glass. Determined to see what this fascinating message was that had riveted George to the spot, I read:

The use of alcohol lamps, sterno lamps, and all other flame-producing appliances, as well as electric devices, is positively forbidden.

"That makes it rather tough for you, doesn't it," I said, "with all your flame-producing appliances? Shall we go to another hotel?"

George said nothing, but went to get his hat. I sauntered over to the door to wait for him, but my eye was caught by a neatly-printed sign which, although I knew that it would contain nothing which could possibly affect me personally, I was utterly unable to keep from reading:

In accepting garments for valet service it is thoroughly

understood that they do not contain money, jewelry, or any other articles of value, and, consequently ——

"Come on, come on!" said George. "We're late now!"

"Just a minute!" It was I this time who had the pre-occupied air. It was I whose eyes were glued to the tiny card and who could not leave until I had finished its stirring message ——

——*consequently the hotel's management or any of its staff will not be held responsible for the return of anything but the garments originally delivered.*

"O. K.!" I announced briskly. "Come on!"

But George had found another sign on the wall by the door. This time we both read it together in silence.

Do not turn thumb latch when leaving room. Door is self-locking. Use thumb latch only when in room.

"What thumb latch is that?" George said, looking over the assortment of latches and catches on the door.

"This is it here," I said, equally engrossed.

"Don't turn it!" cried George, in terror. "It says not to turn it."

"Who's turning it?" I snapped back. "I was just seeing how it worked. Who would want to turn it, anyway?"

"You can't tell," replied George. "Somebody might have this room who had a terrible hunch for turning thumb latches. A hotel has to deal with a lot of strange eggs."

"What would happen if you did turn it?" I asked.

George shuddered. "It might transform the whole hotel into a pumpkin under our very feet," he said, in a low voice.

"Don't be so jumpy," I said, impatiently. That sort

of thing belongs to the Middle Ages—and, besides, it used to happen only at the stroke of midnight."

"What time is it now?" asked George. He was in a cold sweat.

"A quarter to five," I said, looking at my watch. "There's not much sense in going to that four-o'clock date now."

George agreed, so we took off our hats and spent the rest of the afternoon roaming about the room, reading signs to our hearts' content. We were rewarded by several even duller notices than the ones we had already studied and by a good 15 minutes over the 21 provisions of Act 146 of the state Legislature making it compulsory for the management of all inns, hotels, and boarding houses to maintain a safe in the office for the reception of valuables belonging to the guests.

"That's an old one," said George. "I've read that before."

"It's good, though," I said. "It always makes great reading. After all, old notices are best."

So we had dinner sent up to the room in order to complete our reading of the hotel laundry list (George flying into a rage at the charge of 75 cents for "dressing sacques") and, by bedtime, had cleaned up the entire supply of printed matter and were well into the Atlantic City telephone book.

If the hotels want to go still further in their campaigns to make their rooms interesting for their guests, I would suggest the introduction of a sort of treasure hunt for each room. On each door could be tacked a little legend saying something like: "I can be found by going (1) to the top of the possession of an old English queen (2) under an article, beginning with 'W,' highly prized by astronomers (3) between two Indian wigwam attachments (4) underneath an American revolutionary firearm."

The guest could then spend his evenings trying to figure out these hiding places and perhaps emerge richer by a cigarette lighter or one of those face cloths done up in tissue paper envelopes which the hotels are so crazy to have you take away. It wouldn't be so much the value of the prize as the fun of finding it, and it would serve the purpose which seems to be the aim of all modern hostelries—namely: to keep the guests out of the open air and to prevent them from going home.

The Sunday Menace

I AM not a gloomy man by nature, nor am I easily depressed. I always say that, no matter how much it looks as if the sun were never going to stop shining and no matter how long the birds carry on their seemingly incessant chatter, there is always a good sleet storm just around the corner and a sniffly head cold in store for those who will only look for it. You can't keep Old Stepmother Nature down for long.

But I frankly see no way out of the problem of Sunday afternoon. For centuries Sunday afternoon has been Old Nell's Curse among the days of the week. Sunday morning may be cheery enough, with its extra cup of coffee and litter of Sunday newspapers, but there is always hanging over it the ominous threat of 3 P. M., when the sun gets around to the back windows and Life stops dead in its tracks. No matter where you are—in China, on the high seas, or in a bird's nest—about 3 o'clock in the afternoon a pall descends over all the world and people everywhere start trying to think of something to do. You might as well try to think of something to do in the death house at Sing Sing, however, because, even if you do it, where does it get you? It is still Sunday afternoon.

The Blue Jeebs begin to drift in along about dessert at Sunday dinner. The last three or four spoonfuls of ice cream somehow lose their flavor and you begin crumbling up your cake instead of eating it. By the time you have finished coffee there is a definite premonition that before long, maybe in 40 or 50 minutes, you will be told some bad news, probably involving the death of several favorite people, maybe even yourself. This feeling gives way to one of resignation. What is there to live for, anyway? At this point, your dessert begins to disagree with you.

On leaving the dining room and wandering aimlessly into the living room (living room indeed; there will be precious little living done in that room this afternoon), every one begins to yawn. The drifts of Sunday papers on the floor which looked so cozy before dinner now are just depressing reminders of the transitory nature of human life. Uncle Ben makes for the sofa and promptly drops off into an unattractive doze. The children start quarreling among themselves and finally involve the grownups in what threatens to be a rather nasty brawl.

"Why don't you go out and play?" some one asks.

"Play what?" is their retort, and a good one, too.

This brings up the whole question of what to do and there is a half-hearted attempt at thinking on the part of the more vivacious members of the party. Somebody goes to the window and looks out. He goes back to his chair, and somebody else wanders over to another window and looks out there, pressing the nose against the pane and breathing absent-mindedly against the glass. This has practically no effect on the situation.

In an attempt to start conversation, a garrulous one says, "Heigh-ho!" This falls flat, and there is a long silence while you look through the pile of newspapers to see if you missed anything in the morning's perusal.

You even read the ship news and the book advertisements.

"This life of Susan B. Anthony looks as if it might be a pretty good book," you say.

"What makes you think so?" queries Ed crossly. Ed came out to dinner because he was alone in town, and now wishes he hadn't. He is already thinking up an excuse to get an early train back.

There being no good reason why you think that the life of Susan B. Anthony might be interesting, you say nothing. You didn't really think that it might be interesting, anyway.

A walk is suggested, resulting in groans from the rest of the group. The idea of bridge arouses only two out of the necessary four to anything resembling enthusiasm. The time for the arrival of Bad News is rapidly approaching and by now it is pretty fairly certain to involve death. The sun strikes in through the window and you notice that the green chair needs reupholstering. The rug doesn't look any too good, either. What's the use, though? There would be no sense in getting a lot of new furniture when every one is going to be dead before long, anyway.

It is a funny thing about the quality of the sunshine on a Sunday afternoon. On other days it is just sunshine and quite cheery in its middle-class way. But on Sunday afternoon it takes on a penetrating harshness which does nothing but show up the furniture. It doesn't make any difference where you are. You may be hanging around the Busy Bee lunch in Hongkong or polishing brass on a yacht in the North Sea; you may be out tramping across the estate of one of the vice-presidents of a big trust company or teaching Indians to read in Arizona. The Sunday afternoon sunlight makes you dissatisfied with everything it hits. It has got to be stopped.

When the automobile came in it looked as if the Sunday afternoon problem was solved. You could climb in at the back door of the old steamer and puff out into the country, where at least you couldn't hear people playing "Narcissus" on the piano several houses away. (People several houses away are always playing "Narcissus" on the piano on Sunday afternoons. If there is one sound that is typical of Sunday afternoon, it is that of a piano being played several houses away.) It is true, of course, that even out in the country, miles away from everything, you could always tell that it was Sunday afternoon by the strange behavior of the birds, but you could at least pick out an open field and turn somersaults (first taking the small change out of your pockets), or you could run head-on into a large oak, causing insensibility. At least, you could in the early days of automobiling.

But, as soon as everybody got automobiles, the first thing they did naturally was to try to run away from Sunday afternoon, with the result that every country road within a hundred miles of any city has now taken the place of the old-time county fair, without the pleasure of the cattle and the jam exhibits. Today the only difference between Sunday afternoon in the city and Sunday afternoon in the country is that, in the country, you don't know the people who are on your lap.

Aside from the unpleasantness of being crowded in with a lot of strangers on a country road and not knowing what to talk about during the long hours while the

212

I really have no remedy for Sunday afternoons

automobiles are waiting to move ahead, there is the actual danger of an epidemic. Supposing some one took a child out riding in the country on Sunday and while they were jammed in line with hundreds of thousands of other pleasure riders the child came down with tonsilitis. There she would be, a carrier of disease, in contact with at least two-thirds of the population, giving off germs right and left and perhaps starting an epidemic which would sweep the country before the crowds could get back to their homes and gargle. Subways and crowded tenements have long been recognized as breeding grounds for afflictions of the nose and throat. Are country roads on Sunday afternoons to be left entirely without official regulation?

I really have no remedy for Sunday afternoon, at least none that I have any confidence in. The only one that might work would be to rearrange the week in your own mind so that Sunday afternoon falls on Saturday. Now, Saturday afternoon is as cheery as Sunday afternoon is depressing. Perhaps we might try taking a day from some week, let us say a Wednesday which wouldn't matter, then Saturday would be Sunday and Sunday would be Monday. This would do away with all that problem of what to do on Sunday afternoon, because there are always plenty of things to do on Saturday. And you would get the benefit of Saturday afternoon sunshine, which is really delightful. Sunday afternoon sunshine would then wreak its havoc on Monday afternoon and you would be working anyway and might not notice it.

Of course, this system would be complicated unless everybody else would agree to make the same rearrangement in the week, and that might take quite a long time to bring about. If you were making a date for, let us say, Friday morning, you would have to say, "That would be Thursday morning of your week," and perhaps people would get irritated at that. In fact, word might get around that you were a little irresponsible and your business might drop off. Personally, a little slump in business would not be too great a price for me to pay for having Sunday fall on Saturday, but I don't suppose that I could sell the idea to many of you money-mad Americans. I may have to be a lone pioneer in the thing and perhaps be jeered at as Fulton was jeered at. All right, go ahead and jeer.

But, until the thing is in good running order, there will have to be some suggestions as to what to do on Sunday afternoon as we have it now. I can do no more than hint at them, but if there is one among them which appeals to you in outline, I will be glad to take it up with you in more detail.

First, I would suggest setting fire to the house along about 1:30 P. M. If the fire were nursed along, it would cause sufficient excitement to make you forget what day it was, at least until it was time to turn on the lights for the evening. Or you might go down into the cellar right after dinner and take the furnace apart, promising yourself to have it put together again by supper time. Here, at least, the sunlight couldn't get at you. Or you could rent a diver's suit and go to the nearest body of water and spend the afternoon tottering about under the surface, picking sea anemone and old bits of wreckage.

The method which I myself have tried with considerable success and little expense, however, is to buy a small quantity of veronal at the nearest druggist's, put it slyly in my coffee on Saturday night, and then bundle off to bed. When you wake up on Monday morning you may not feel crisp, but Sunday will be over.

And that, I take it, is what we are after.

One Set of French Dishes

LAST summer when I was in France, I bought a set
of dishes.* They were just simple earthenware
dishes, such as used to have "For a Good Dog" lettered
on them, but as they were made in a little town up back
in the mountains near the Mediterranean, they seemed
to be rather smart. They cost something like three cents
apiece and were a bright blue. I now think that we made
a mistake in buying them.

As there were perhaps forty pieces in all, including
a large bowl which the old man said was for soup, it
seemed impractical to try to jam them all in a trunk
with the rest of the knicknacks and even less practical to
carry them in our hands with our umbrellas and everything. So we asked the old man if he would think up
some way of putting them in a barrel and sending them
to America by freight. He said *"Oui, oui!"* which we
figured out to mean that he would. And he evidently
did.

That was three months ago. Today I got a notice
from the Custom House saying that there was a bbl.
on the good ship "Hannoy" for me. The only bbl. that
I can think of which would take a ship like the "Hannoy" is a bbl. of dishes. I don't suppose that anyone
would be sending me a bbl. of beer, because it is pretty

* The reader will doubtless recall this curious American custom—
may perhaps have succumbed to it himself—which was prevalent
back in the days when steamers still plied the ocean.—Editor's Note.

well known around France that I don't drink. Certainly not French beer. The notice said for me to put my things right on and come down to the dock and claim my goods, otherwise they couldn't answer for what would happen to the bbl. But somehow I don't think that I will.

For in the same mail came a big, official-looking sheet, colored orange, with lots of stamps on it and about six hundred and fifty thousand French words closely printed. It says at the top *"Compagnie Française de Navigation à Vapeur"* and that means, according to a very hasty translation which I have thrown together "French Company of Navigation to Steam." These French are very quick at picking up new inventions and here is Robert Fulton scarcely cold in his grave before we find them navigating to steam. The rest of the document is not so clear.

The only typewritten words on the sheet are "Hannoy" and *"I cassie poterie rustique."* This evidently means my dishes. But the rest of the reading-matter is rather cryptic. There is so much of it, in the first place, and, at the bottom, it says that *"le chargeur"* (which must be I, unless it is the old man in Biotte) declares to have taken cognizance of the clauses printed above and accepts them. (All this is in French, mind you, but I get that part all right.) I am not so sure, however, that I want to accept the clauses printed above.

In the first place, as I read it over, the whole thing seems to be a threat. I have evidently placed myself under suspicion by shipping a bbl. of *"poterie rustique"* to America. Spelling out the words in my rough, untutored way, I seem to detect a great many penalties. I don't

219

know whether the French penalize you merely for ship-ping goods to another country, but I wouldn't put it past them. Mind you, I think that the Germans treated the French very badly in 1914 and I never had any use for the Kaiser, but I would not put it past the French to slip in a dirty penalty now and then if they got a chance. And on this orange bill-of-lading of mine, I seem to detect a slight plot to have my head cut off in the Place de la Concorde.

Under a paragraph marked *"Clause penale"* I make out several words which lead me to believe that if I go down to the dock to claim my goods I make myself liable to life-imprisonment and the amputation of one leg. This may be wrong, but that's the way I translate it. I am not so sure about its being a leg that I am to have amputated, and I am not sure that, if it is a leg, I am to have it amputated, but it sounds like that. Now I am not going down to any dock just for a bbl. of dishes and run into anything like that. And I am certain about the other phrase being "life-imprisonment." That is enough in itself.

The word *"fret"* keeps occurring in practically every sentence, and, while I am not silly enough to think that it really means what the English word "fret" means, it has an ugly sound nevertheless. According to this docu-ment, my *fret* has to be examined and, if it doesn't suit the *fret*-examiners the *Tribune de Commerce de Mar-seille* will meet in a body and decide what to do with it. As I make it out they can take my *fret* and either (a) burn it (b) drown it or (c) eat it themselves. This is going to make it very awkward for me, not even know-ing what my *fret* is. Furthermore, I can't be running over to Marseilles and back every few days just to answer questions for their old *Tribune de Commerce*. If they want to examine my *fret*, they can come over here and do it. I am a busy man.

There seem to be other clauses in my bill-of-lading which would indicate that I would just be a fool to go anywhere near the freight dock after those dishes. Under the head of *Litiges*, which ought to mean something about litigation, I find that a lot of talk is made about an item called *"avaries."* In case there happens to be an *avarie* in your *fret* you are in for all kinds of trouble and may possibly have to live on the second floor of the Custom House all the rest of your life. At least, that is what the French would seem to say.

Now I don't know what *avaries* are, but it looks to me as if they were either misers or bird-houses. By a process of elimination we may decide that there probably wouldn't be any misers in a shipment of goods from Southern France, not because there aren't any misers in Southern France but because they most likely could not be induced to get into a crate for such a long trip. So we may safely say that *avaries* are not misers. (It would be just the way things work out now for me to get down to the dock and find a whole bunch of misers hidden in among my dishes.) But it is much more likely that *avaries* are bird-houses, with birds in them. And if anyone is so unfortunate as to have a bird-house discovered in his bill of goods, he is, according to this paper, as good as in chains right there.

I have no reason to suppose that the old man in Biotte slipped any bird-houses in my pottery when he was packing it, but how am I to know? He was a pretty nasty old man and didn't like me at all. I remember now that when I asked him if the tea-cups were to hang in the window with ferns in them, he gave me a very dirty look and I thought at the time, "If there is anything that Grandpa can do to make things hard for you, he is going to do it." Now what would be simpler than for him to have put a bird-house right in with that big souptureen, knowing very well that it would cause me trouble? All French potters who use marine freight at all must know this orange-colored sheet backward and must know that anyone caught with a bird-house (*or miser*) in his shipment is going to be subjected to all the indignities which the *Code de Procédure Civile* can think up. He could have fitted the bird-house with a set of love-birds or parrakeets which would be very noisy and call attention to themselves the minute the *fret*-investigators came anywhere near them. He might even have put in a parrot which would scream out, "Look, look! Here I am!" or *"Avarie! avarie!"* He could have done *anything*, and the more I think about the way he looked at me the more I think that he probably did.

So I think that I will just tuck the orange sheet and the notice from the freight office in the back of my drawer and forget about them. The men on the dock can probably find some use for my dishes, although I doubt if they would like them so blue. We really have enough dishes at home already and another set would not be worth all the penalties that I would be liable to by claiming them. I have several more years left before I have to start walking with a cane, and I don't want to spend them on the second floor of the Marseilles Custom House or languishing in a French jail.

Just for curiosity's sake, however, I must look up and see whether *avaries* are misers or bird-houses.

A Dark Horse in British Sports*

I HAD just about decided that I was getting too old for athletic sports, what with my left knee bending backward just as easily as it does forward and my face getting purple when I so much as lift an arm, but now everything is different. I am going in training again. And it is the Travel Association of Great Britain and Ireland which has done this for me.

The T. A. of G. B. and I. has sent me a pamphlet called "Calendar of Historic and Important Events of the Year," and it is full of the peachiest things. A lot of them are aimed at the indoor trade, such as the Carnation Show on November twenty-sixth in the Royal Horticultural Hall (I'm afraid I can't make the Carna-

---

* The editors can only regret that world conditions, unforeseen at the time of writing, will prevent Mr. Benchley's ever becoming known as the champion of the Westminster School Shrove Tuesday Pancake Tossing Contest—an event he was so happily anticipating.—Editor's Note.

tion Show and I am simply sick about it) or the Scottish Home Life Exhibition (whee-e-e!) at Edinburgh in April. These things which are held in halls are too sedentary. I must be up and about.

For me, there seem to be countless forms of healthful exercise available in the British Isles this year. In September there will be "tossing the caber" at the Braemar Highland Gathering; on April twenty-second there will be "street football" at Workington, Cumberland, "played through the streets of the town with hundreds of players on each side"; in June there will be the Uphellya at Lerwick, Shetland, and on Shrove Tuesday, Westminster School will indulge in its rite of "tossing the pancake."

As Shrove Tuesday is nearest at hand, let us get down to training for "tossing the pancake" first. I am taking it for granted that "tossing the pancake" corresponds to our American "snapping the cookies," and, if it does, I am in pretty good training right now. A little more control in the matter of direction, and I am set for the contest at Westminster. I may not be quite so young as the boys who go to school there, but I have given my system some pretty tough treatment in the past ten years and there ought to be no difficulty in keeping up with the sickliest of them. I once held the trans-Atlantic cookie-putting (or snapping) cup and lost it the next year only to a man who had a complication of other troubles, which more or less rendered him a professional. For an amateur, otherwise in good health (which ought to be a specification in any cookie-snapping, or pancake-tossing competition), I have every confidence that I can hold my own against the field. The only part about this Westminster meeting that I don't like is its

I would feel that sooner or later he would turn into a fairy prince and whisk me off to the moon

coming on Shrove Tuesday. I usually have other things to do on Shrove Tuesday.

I would know more how to train for the Lerwick "Uphellya" if I knew what they did there. It sounds a little unpleasant. I rather imagine that some fighting goes on and maybe a little preliminary drinking. I might enter my name for the preliminary drinking and then see how I liked the rest of it. After the preliminary drinking, however, I probably would like—and enter—anything. That might be bad, as there are a lot of things which I really shouldn't enter. I don't know much about the residents of Lerwick, or what they are likely to do at an "Uphellya," but so long as it doesn't involve running more than ten yards or vaulting, I guess that I can keep up. I never could vault, even in my heyday (1846-1847), owing to a third leg which always seemed to appear just as I was about to clear the bar and drag about three inches too low. I never could find that leg after the vaulting was over, and it is something I would rather not talk about, if you don't mind.

Of course, taking place on the island of Shetland, the whole thing may be done on ponies, which wouldn't be so good. I know that it sounds silly, but I have always been just a little afraid of Shetland ponies. No horse would be so small as that unless he had something up his sleeve to make up for it. It isn't natural for a horse to be so small. I wouldn't get on one for $1,000,000 (well anyway, for $5) because I would always feel that, sooner or later, he would grow big on me or turn into a fairy prince and whisk me off to the moon. Perhaps I haven't communicated to you my feeling about Shetland ponies, but it is a pretty subtle one, and if you haven't already got it for yourself, I could talk all night without making you understand. When I have said that, for grown-up horses, they are *too small*, I have said everything. And if the Shetland "Uphellya" is held on Shetland ponies, they can scratch me.

The "street football" in Workington, Cumberland, with hundreds of players on each side rushing through the streets of the town, sounds pretty uninteresting. I don't think that I shall even enter that. It is the sort of thing which sounds like a lot of fun when you are planning it, but which works out to be a terrible flop. In the first place, the streets of Workington can't be very wide, as none of the streets is wide in an English town. This means that only about five or six men can possibly be in line from one wall to another. In other words, there are going to be about 192 players on each side who have nothing to do but giggle and push each other about. This is going to be not only dull but bad for the morale. Before the game has been on for fifteen minutes those who are unwilling nonparticipants are going to get tired of pushing each other about and are going to slide into the nearest pub and wait for the thing to be over. Pretty soon those in the front line are going to realize what fools they are making of themselves by kicking a football around when they might be with their team-mates in a nice warm pub, and they are going to stop, too. This will leave just the football rolling by itself in the streets and all the women and visitors sitting up in windows, wondering where the two teams are. My suggestion would be that they save time by getting the two teams in the pub right at the start, and letting the women and visitors kick the ball about. My interest in it is purely academic, however, as I shall not be there.

The last event for which I have to train is the one held

at the Braemar Highland Gathering in September, "tossing the caber." I have asked several sporting goods dealers if they have a caber and they have told me that they are all out. There seems to be a big run on cabers this season. As I remember it, a caber is either a pole about the size of a flagstaff or a small animal like an ant-eater. In either case, I would not be particularly crazy about tossing it. I seem to have seen pictures of men in kilts hoisting a great pole into the air, but never any pictures of its landing; so I don't know whether you actually throw it or just stand there and hold it up until somebody comes along and tells you to drop it. Hoisting the pole might be all right, but I would rather not wear the kilts, if it is all the same to the committee. I once wore kilts to a fancy dress party and I am still blushing over what happened.

I rather think that my best event will be tossing the pancake at Westminster School on Shrove Tuesday. I am not making a book on it, and I don't want to lead any of my friends into betting, but I will say this much: if you have a little cash that you want to invest and will take a fifteen-to-one bet (I am a dark horse in West-minster and the favorite, I understand, is a boy with a very weak stomach who won last year) you could do worse than to send your money to "Duggie," the London bookmaker who advertises on the back pages of the London weeklies, with instructions for him to do what he thinks best, but, if possible, to slip it in very quietly on "Daisy Bob" (my stable name).

At any rate, I shall be back in athletic circles again and getting exercise. I can never thank the Travel Association of Great Britain and Ireland enough.

The Stranger within our Gates

ONE of the problems of child education which is not generally included in books on the subject is the Visiting Schoolmate. By this is meant the little friend whom your child brings home for the holidays. What is to be done with him, the Law reading as it does?

He is usually brought home because his own home is in Nevada, and if he went 'way out there for Christmas he would no sooner get there than he would have to turn right around and come back—an ideal arrangement on the face of it. But there is something in the idea of a child away from home at Christmas-time that tears at the heart-strings, and little George is received into the bosom of your family with open arms and a slight catch in the throat. Poor little nipper! He must call up his parents by telephone on Christmas Day; they will miss him so. (It later turns out that even when George's parents lived in Philadelphia he spent his vacations with friends, his parents being no fools.)

For the first day George is a model of politeness. "George is a nice boy," you say to your son; "I wish you knew more like him." "George seems to be a very manly little chap for fourteen," your wife says after the boys have gone to bed. "I hope that Bill is impressed." Bill, as a matter of fact, does seem to have caught some of little George's gentility and reserve, and the hope for his future which had been practically abandoned is revived again under his schoolmate's influence.

230

The first indication that George's stay is not going to be a blessing comes at the table, when, with confidence born of one day's association, he announces flatly that he does not eat potatoes, lamb or peas, the main course of the meal consisting of potatoes, lamb and peas. "Perhaps you would like an egg, George?" you suggest. "I hate eggs," says George, looking out the window while he waits for you to hit on something that he does like.

"I'm afraid you aren't going to get much to eat tonight, then, George," you say. "What is there for dessert?"

"A nice bread pudding with raisins," says your wife.

George, at the mention of bread pudding, gives what is known as "the bird," a revolting sound made with the tongue and lower lip. "I can't eat raisins anyway," he adds, to be polite. "They make me come out in a rash."

"Ah-h! The old raisin-rash," you say. "Well, we'll keep you away from raisins, I guess. And just what is it that you can eat, George? You can tell me. I am your friend."

Under cross-examination it turns out that George can eat beets if they are cooked just right, a rare species of eggplant grown only in Nevada, and all the ice cream in the world. He will also cram down a bit of cake now and then for manners' sake.

All this would not be so bad if it were not for the fact that, coincidentally with refusing the lamb, George

criticizes your carving of it. "My father carves lamb across the grain instead of the way you do," he says, a little crossly.

"Very interesting," is your comment.

"My father says that only old ladies carve straight down like that," he goes on.

The presents turn out to be things he already has, only his are better

"Well, well," you say pleasantly between your teeth, "That makes me out sort of an old lady, doesn't it?"

"Perhaps you have a different kind of lamb in Nevada," you suggest, hacking off a large chunk. (You have never carved so badly.) "A kind that feeds on your special kind of eggplant."

"We don't have lamb very often," says George. "Mostly squab and duck."

"You stick to squab and duck, George," you say, "and it will be just dandy for that rash of yours. Here take this and like it!" And you toss him a piece of lamb which, oddly enough, is later found to have disappeared from his plate.

It also turns out later that George's father can build sailboats, make a monoplane that will really fly, repair a broken buzzer and imitate birds, none of which you can do and none of which you have ever tried to do, having given it to be understood that they *couldn't* be done. You begin to hate George's father almost as much as you do George.

"I suppose your father writes articles for the magazines, too, doesn't he, George?" you ask sarcastically.

"Sure," says George with disdain. "He does that Sundays—Sunday afternoons."

"Yes, sir," says George.

This just about cleans up George so far as you are concerned, but there are still ten more days of vacation. And during these ten days your son Bill is induced by George to experiment with electricity to the extent of blowing out all the fuses in the house and burning the cigarette-lighter out of the sedan; he is also inspired to call the cook a German spy who broils babies, to insult several of the neighbors' little girls to the point of tears and reprisals, and to refuse spinach. You know that Bill didn't think of these things himself, as he never could have had the imagination.

On Christmas Day all the little presents that you got for George turn out to be things that he already has, only his are better. He incites Bill to revolt over the question of where the tracks to the electric train are to be placed (George maintaining that in his home they run through his father's bathroom, which is the only sensible place for tracks to run). He breaks several of little Barbara's more fragile presents and says that she broke them herself by not knowing how to work them. And the day ends with George running a high temperature and coming down with mumps, necessitating a quarantine and enforced residence in your house for a month.

This is just a brief summary of the Visiting Schoolmate problem. Granted that every child should have a home to go to at Christmas, could there not be some sort of state subsidy designed to bring their own homes on to such children as are unable to go home themselves? On such a day each home should be a sanctuary, where only members of the tribe can gather and overeat and quarrel. Outsiders just complicate matters, especially when outsiders cannot be spanked.

One-Two-Three-Four

IF I grow up to be a puny, under-developed sort of man, with a narrow chest and no eyelashes, it will be because modern civilization has made it so difficult for me to get any exercise. Not that modern civilization will give a darn.

I try and try to find some means of sending a little of that rare old Benchley blood coursing through my veins at even a slightly faster pace than a float in a Carnival of Roses parade. I don't ask for much of my blood in the way of speed. Just to have it keep moving and not hang around getting in the way of food-particles and other things that may want to *get* somewhere is all I need. But I can't seem to get any exercise. And, without exercise, the only way you can stimulate your circulation is to have somebody come in and slap you all over. Not for me, thank you! I still have my pride left.

About once a year I come to the realization that unless I get some form of exercise pretty soon I will have little ferns and things growing out on me; so I make out a schedule of quick, darting movements to be made at various times of the day, usually just before getting into the tub in the morning. Now other men seem to be able to find space enough in their room to do a daily dozen or two without banging their elbows against furniture, but I am not so fortunate. No matter how big my room is and no matter how simple my drill, I always bang my elbows against a wall or a bureau at one time or another. I believe that I could stand in the middle of the floor of the room in which they signed the Versailles Treaty, and within a minute and a half be whacking an arm or knee against a wall or one of those big glass chandeliers.

I think that one of my chief troubles in this respect is that I hitch sideways very slowly as I work. I know that this is true when I am lying on the floor in one of those exercises which call for lying on the back and waving the legs aloft. I can lie on my back in the middle of an enormous room, miles from any one of the four walls, and, by the time I have got my legs up and down six times, I will have hitched myself in a diagonal line to the right until I give myself a nasty crack against the baseboard. If it were a part of the drill to do that I probably couldn't do it with such precision. I don't understand how it is done to this day. In fact, I used to think that perhaps the wall moved in toward *me* instead of my moving toward the wall, but my knowledge of physics came to my aid and made me realize that such a thing was probably impossible. I hitch, and that is all that there is to it.

Of course, this makes it unfeasible to try any of those exercises on the bed. There was a time when I had a very scratchy rug in my room and, rather than lie down on it and get burrs in my back, I tried lying on the bed when it came time to wave my legs. Although this was a much pleasanter way of doing it, I found that my tendency to hitch sideways had me off on the floor in no time, once in a while hurting myself rather badly.

Another disadvantage to doing the supine exercises on a bed was that I found myself going back to sleep in the middle of them. If I had been out late the night before and had a disinclination to getting up anyway, I found that as soon as I got back on the bed to do the leg-work I was dozing off again, sometimes with my legs in the air. There is something about the feeling of the pillow under your head and the soft mattress under your back that makes exercise seem like a hollow mockery, and the last time I did it I went right back to sleep again and slept until noon. So *that* is out.

This inability to find any place in my own house in which to do morning setting-up rather starts the day off badly. I might be able to get back into shape again if I could work at it in the morning, but since this is evidently out of the question I am forced to get my exercise during the day. And you know what "during the day" is. It is *never*.

Walking to work is supposed to be an excellent form of body movement and I suppose that if I worked out in the country somewhere, filling silos or worrying sheep, I could get a good three or four miles in on my way to work. But most of the time I work right in the room next to where I sleep, and while on a good brisk morning I can easily walk it, it doesn't do an awful lot for my circulation. Eight good long steps and I am at my desk. I suppose that I *might* walk in and out of my bed-room and work-room two or three hundred times before sitting down to work, but, even if nobody saw me at it, I would feel pretty silly. And, even then, I doubt if it would do me much good, what with bumping into chairs and tables and stopping to read the morning paper every few feet. So walking to work is out. And the day is half over.

Walking to lunch suggests itself as the next possibility, but I very seldom eat lunch. And even when I do go out for a bite there are so many other people walking to and from lunch that I keep slipping off the curb and into the gutter every few feet to get out of their way. I suppose that I *could* elbow along the way a great many of them do and make *other* people step off into the gutter, but somehow it seems easier not to put

up the fight. I might, when I go out to lunch, put on a sweater and sneakers and run at a dog-trot up Fifth Avenue, thus giving people the idea that I really mean business, but then, by the time I got to lunch, I would be all red and wet and not a very good companion I am afraid.

In fact, walking as an exercise when one lives in the city is pretty unsatisfactory, in the first place because you have to keep stopping to let traffic go by, or if you are so bent on walking that you *don't* stop, you are going to get a large town-car on the hip and *then* where is your physical condition? You can run up and down stairs in

By the time I got to lunch I would be all red and wet and not a very good companion

a twenty-story building if you like, but people who do that are always dropping dead, and that's no fun either.

Every once in a while I join some gymnasium class composed of business men who have just begun to realize that they can't get rid of that extra-waist simply by tightening their belts. I have given this up because it always brings on some serious illness in me. The last time I went to a class and bounced around with bankers and advertising men, I came down with a complete disintegration of the joints and had to be all taken apart and put together again. It seemed that I had been storing up poison in my system for years, but so long as I walked gently on tip-toe and did nothing to stir it up, I was fine. The minute I began jarring it by bounding around on mats and waving my arms, all the poison got to circulating through my system and got shaken into places where it never would have thought of going before, with the result that I had to have a man come up from the garage with a blow-torch to get it out of my joints. It was the exercise that did it. If I had left the poison alone where it was hurting no one, I would have been all right.

Hand-ball is another form of after-office-hours exercise which I cannot indulge in, chiefly because it bores the living life out of me and I don't like the air in a hand-ball court anyway. When I was even a smaller boy than I am now, we used to have a cave in my cellar which extended out under the sidewalk and into which we used to crawl with candles and smoke Cubebs. After a good rainy spell, this cave, with the damp candle and Cubeb smoke, was the nearest thing to a hand-ball court that I can remember. I could fling myself about in a hand-ball court all day, even with the windows wide open, and get no more physical benefit than I used to get from crawling around in that hole under the side-walk of King Street. A lot of men seem to do it, and, while I wouldn't go so far as to say that they *look* any better for it, they evidently enjoy it. I guess I must be made of rather finer stuff.

Perhaps that is the trouble anyway. Maybe Nature didn't intend me to exercise. She certainly doesn't make it very easy for me to. It might very well be that I am more the dreamer type, designed to lie on one elbow on a rock in the Mediterranean and evolve little fancies without ever so much as raising a finger. In this case I should have to have my food brought out to me from some good caterer on shore, as shell-fish poison me. There must be some people who do not have to take exercise, and I might as well be one of them. It would fit into my scheme of life much better.

But I do like starchy foods. And there we are, right back where we started from.

Ask Me a Question

PROFESSORS in our universities are getting awfully nosey of late. They are always asking questions or sending out questionnaires inquiring into your private life. I can remember the day when all that a professor was supposed to do was to mark "C minus" on students' examination papers and then go home to tea. Nowadays they seem to feel that they must know just how much we (outside the university) eat, what we do with our spare time, and how we like our eggs. I, for one, am inclined not to tell any more. I already have filled in enough stuff on questionnaires to get myself divorced or thrown into jail.

A particularly searching series of questions has just come from an upstate university trying to find out about my sleeping habits. The director of the psychological laboratory wants to know a lot of things which, if I were to give them out, would practically put me in the position of sleeping in John Wanamaker's window. I would have no more privacy than Irvin Cobb.

The first question is a simple one: "How many hours do you sleep each night, on the average?"

Well, professor, that would be hard to say. I might add "and what's it to you?" but I suppose there must be some reason for wanting to know. I can't imagine any subject of less general interest than the number of hours I sleep each night on the average. No one has ever given a darn before, and I must say that I am rather touched at this sudden display of interest on the part of a stranger. Perhaps if I were to tell him that I hardly sleep at all he would come down and read to me.

But I would like to bet that the professor gets a raft of answers. If there is one thing that people like to talk about it is their sleeping habits. Just get a group started telling how much or how little they sleep each night and you will get a series of personal anecdotes which will put the most restless member of the party to sleep in no time.

"Well, it's a funny thing about me," one will say. "I get to bed, we'll say, at 11:30, and I go to sleep the minute my head hits the pillow and sleep right through until 7:30."

He will be interrupted at this point by some one who insists on having it known that the night before he heard the clock strike 2, 3, and 4. (People always seem to take a great deal of pride in having heard the clock strike 2, 3, and 4. You will seldom find one who admits having slept soundly all through the night. Just as a man will never admit that the suit he has on is new, so is he loath to confess that he is a good sleeper. I don't understand it, but, as I am getting pretty old now, I don't much care.)

You will be lucky if, in an experience meeting of this kind, you don't start some one off telling the dream he had a few nights ago.

"It was the darndest thing," some one will say, as the rest pay no attention, but try to think up dreams they themselves have had recently, "it was the darndest thing. I seemed to be in a sort of big hall, only it wasn't exactly a hall either; it was more of a rink or schoolhouse. It seemed that Harry was there and all of a sudden instead of Harry it was Lindbergh. Well, so we all were going to a football game or something and I had on my old gray suit, except that it had wheels on it ——"

By this time everybody is engaged in lighting cigarettes or looking at newspapers or even talking to some one else in a low tone of voice, and the narrator of the dream has practically no one to listen to him except the unfortunate who happens to be sitting next. But he doesn't seem to care and goes right on, until he has finished. There is a polite murmur of "What had you been eating?" or "That certainly was a corker," and then some one else starts. The professor who sent this questionnaire will have to watch out for this sort of thing or he will be swamped.

The whole list is just a temptation to garrulousness. Question No. 3, for example, is likely to get people started on an hour's personal disclosure. "Do you notice ill effects the day after sleeping on a train?" is the way it is worded.

Well, now take me for example. I'm glad you asked that, professor. I do notice ill effects the day after sleeping on a train. I notice, in the first place, that I haven't got my underthings buttoned correctly.

Dressing in a Pullman berth is, at best, a temporary form of arraying oneself, but if I happen to have to go right from the train to my engagement without going first to a hotel and doing the whole thing over again, I find, during the day, that I have buttoned the top button of my running drawers into the bottom buttonhole of my waistcoat and that one whole side of my shirt is clamped, by some mysterious process, half way up my back. This, as the day wears on, exerts a pull on the parts affected until there is grave danger of the whole body becoming twisted to the right, or left, as the case may be. This, in turn, leads to an awkward gait in walking and is likely to cause comment. Of course, if it is a strange town, people may think that you walk that way naturally and, out of politeness, say nothing about it, but among friends you are pretty sure to be accused of affectation or even worse.

Another ill effect, professor, which I feel after having slept on a Pullman (leaving aside the inevitable cold in the head acquired from sleeping with a light brown blanket piled high on one hip), is the strange appearance I present when I take my hat off.

As I am usually the last man in the washroom, I am constantly being harried by the porter, who keeps coming to the door and telling me that the train is pulling out into the yards in three minutes. (It is always three minutes, never less and never, by any chance, more.) Now, with this unpleasant threat hanging over me, I am in no state of mind to make my customary exquisite toilet. I brush my teeth and possibly shave one-half of my face, but almost invariably forget to brush my hair. It is all right going through the station with my hat on, but later in the day, when I come to my business appointments, I notice that I am the object of considerable curious attention from people who do not know me, owing to my hair standing on end during an entire conference or even a luncheon. It is usually laid to my being a writer and of an artistic temperament, but it doesn't help me in a business way.

Now you will see what you got yourself into by merely asking me that one question, professor. I could go on like this for hours, telling about the ill effects I feel the day after sleeping in a Pullman, but maybe you aren't interested any longer. I am afraid I have bored you already.

The next question, however, is likely to start me off again. "Do you usually sleep through the night without awakening?"

It is funny that you should have asked that. I was just about to tell you anyway. Some nights I do, and some nights I don't. I can't be any more explicit than that.

When my little boys were small, I really can't say that I did. Not that they really meant to be mean about it, or did it deliberately, but, as I look back on it, it seems that there was always something. A glass of water was usually the ostensible excuse, but a great many times it turned out to be just a desire on their part to be chummy and have some one to cry with. I would say

249

that, during the infancy of my bairn, my average was something like 10 complete arisings from bed during the night and 15 incomplete ones. By "incomplete" I mean those little starts out of a sound sleep, where one leg is thrust out from under the bedclothes while one waits to see if maybe the disturbance will not die down of its own accord.

These abortive arisings are really just as disturbing to the sleep as the complete ones, and should count as much in any scientific survey. (I do not want to convey the impression that I did all the hopping up during the night. The mother of the boys did her share, but it was a good two-man job on which turns had to be taken. It also depended a lot on which one could the better simulate sleep at the time of the alarm.)

Now that the boys are old enough to get up and get Daddy water when he wants it, things are a little different, but I find that the amount of undisturbed sleep that I get in one night's rest is dependent on so many outside factors that it is almost impossible to make up any statistics on the subject. A great deal of it depends on the neighbors and how much fun they happen to be having. Then there is the question of what tunes I've heard during the day. One good, monotonous tune firmly imbedded in my consciousness will make going to bed just a matter of form.

Two nights ago I retired early for a good rest (my first in nine years), but unfortunately spent seven out of my possible eight hours trying to get "What Is This Thing Called Love?" out of my mind. If I had only known some more of the words it wouldn't have been quite so bad, but one can't go on, hour after hour, mentally singing "What is this thing called love—what is this thing called love—what is this thing called love," without suffering some sort of nervous breakdown. It would have been much better for me to have been walking the streets than lying there in bed, plugging a song for nobody in particular.

It is this sort of thing which makes it difficult to answer Question No. 4. One night I am one way; the next night I am another way.

The only means that I can think of for the professor to employ to get an accurate check-up on my sleeping habits would be for him to come down to my place and sleep on an army cot at the foot of my bed himself. He would have to bring his own blankets, though, as I have hardly enough for myself as it is.

The King's English: Not
Murder but Suicide

BEING by nature and carefully acquired tastes something of an Anglophile, the following rather bitter outburst is going to hurt me more than it hurts England. In fact when, in the old days before I began filling out, I was occasionally told by strangers that I looked as if I might be English, I very often did nothing to correct the impression and even went so far as to throw in a word like "shedule" or "*cem*ent" deliberately to strengthen it. England has no better friend in the world than I am, even though I sometimes appear out of patience. That is because I am tired.

But, royalist though I am at heart, I find myself taking the old musket down from the wall and priming it for a determined stand against the redcoats who continue to assail our right to pronounce words as they are spelled. For years we colonists have submitted meekly to the charge that we speak the English language badly. We know that it is true in a way, that our voices are harsh and loud, that some of us roll our "r's" while others say "boid" and "erl," and we also know that, in the matter of vocabulary we are mere children lisping "cat," "doggie" and "O.K." exclusively. And the knowledge of these shortcomings, together with the venomous scorn with which our English friends point them out, has bred an inferiority in us which is nothing short of craven. We never think of turning on our tormentors and saying "You're not so hot yourselves!"

British nausea at American pronunciation reached an almost active stage after the invasion of England by Hollywood-made talking-pictures. London editorial writers took the matter into their own hands and urged an embargo on American films on the charge of corrupting their youth. They saw the complete degradation of the English language in fifty years if little English children were allowed to listen at their movies to the horrid sound of Americans talking. There was some idea of limiting the sale of tickets to those of his Majesty's subjects who were safely established in the traditional English habits of speech, barring at the door all those in the formative stage. Others would have had the pictorial parts of the films made in Hollywood (since England seemed to be having a little trouble in making any that would sell) but the sound-tracts made in Elstree by strictly British voices, the two being synchronized to produce a picture which might be listened to by English tots without fear of contamination. The whole island was evidently on the verge of a panic such as might arise at the approach of a fleet of cholera-ridden ships up the Thames.

No one in America will deny that many of the beautiful young gentlemen and ladies of Hollywood should never have been called upon to talk. Neither will anyone deny that a large number of American actresses and actors who go to London in the spoken drama might well offend the sensitive British ear. They have offended even the cauliflower ear of New York.

But is England entirely without sin in the matter of language distortion? Might New York never justifiably be distressed by the sounds made by the countless English casts which came over here to earn twice what they could earn at home? Is the frequent confusion in the minds of American audiences as to just what the English actors are saying on the stage due to the fact that our auditory faculties are not attuned to pure English or to the fact that the English actors are not pronouncing the words properly as they are spelled? If spelling means anything at all in the pronunciation of a word, then the English are at fault. If it doesn't, then they are at fault anyway.

Of course, there can be no argument (and let us have this understood at the start, please) over the comparative mellifluousness of English and American speech. Even the most incompetent English actor, coming on the stage briefly to announce the presence below of Lord and Lady Ditherege, gives forth a sound so soft and dulcet as almost to be a bar of music. But sometimes that is all there is. The words are lost in the graceful sweep of the notes. I have heard entire scenes played by English actors (especially juveniles) in which absolutely nothing was distinguishable except a series of musical notes ranging in cadenzas from B to G sharp and back to B again. It is all very pretty, but is it the English language?

This slurring of words into a refined cadence until they cease to be words at all is due partly to the Englishman's disinclination to move his lips. Evidently the lips and teeth are held stationary for the most part, open just wide enough to let in air for breathing (many Englishmen must breathe through their mouths, otherwise they would not breathe at all) with an occasional sharp pursing of the lips on a syllable which does *not* call for pursing the lips. This lethargic attitude toward articulation makes more or less of a fool out of a word which is dependent on pronunciation for its success. It makes a rather agreeable sound of it, but practically eliminates it as an agent for expressing thought.

I am not dealing now with cockney or other perversions of the British manner of speaking, although Englishmen are not so fair as to remember that much of the speech which they call "American" on the stage and in pictures is deliberately vulgarized and harshened by the American actors themselves to imitate gangsters, newspaper reporters, and others of the non-classical group. I am speaking of the more "refayned" type of English actor, and even of the ordinary well-educated Englishman. They distort good old Anglo-Saxon words into mere blobs of sound, eliminating letters and syllables at will. And what they do to *French* words must not be mentioned here because that is not strictly within the range of his thesis. Neither is it important.

But it is safe to predict that a comparative tabulation of words in common use in England and America, analyzed phonetically as pronounced in each country, would give America a startling lead over the mother-country in accuracy. Saying them through the nose, as many Americans do, may not be so pleasant as saying them through the large palate, as many Englishmen do, but the words themselves get a better break and, at least, the integrity of the sentence is preserved.

The time is about ripe for someone to write a skit for an American revue, lasting perhaps three minutes, in which are reproduced the sounds made by a group of English juveniles such as came over here every year in plays of post-war younger-generationism, bounding on and off the stage carrying tennis racquets and giving off exuberance to the point of combustion. If I were writing such a sketch I would open the scene with two or three young gentlemen and ladies lying about on window-seats and porch chairs in careless fashion, with the conversation running something like this:

Wotjuthinkofrehddie?

Hesbeanofflyapsehtletly

Eheaidehntneh-hehesentehnyfethleft

At this point Reggie would come bursting into the room, with his shirt open at the neck, fresh from badminton and would call, swinging his body lithely from the hips:

Elleuhvrybohddyweresahncle?

Things would go on like this for a minute or two with absolutely no word being spoken, just a series of British sounds with a great deal of bounding about and quick, darting movements of the heads and arms. The young men would stand with feet wide apart and hands jammed down into the side pockets of their coats, while the young ladies would stand with their feet not quite so far apart and their hands jammed down into the pockets of their sweaters. It would all have to be played very fast and loosely and might end with their all putting their heads together and doing the thing in harmony, still with no words. Or a canary, which had been hanging in a cage throughout the act, might join in with them until it fell dead from exhaustion. Or almost anything might happen, provided no sense was given to the lines.

Some time ago I heard *Major Barbara* done by an English company. The young man who played Cusins was a particularly vicious example of the songster-actor so prevalent on the English stage. Although I took no notes and am not very good at carrying a tune, I should say that one of his speeches ran something like this: (The key was C sharp and the range was from B to G sharp in an almost continuous cadenza) :

"Eetsnottth'sao ehvmeh seuhl thett trehbles meh; Eh hev seuhld et teuh efften teh care abeht thett. Eh hev seuhld et fereh preuhfessorshep. Eh hev seuhld et tescep beinempressoned feh refusin t'peh texes fer hengmen's reuhps end ehnjust wehrs end things thet ehabheuh. Wot es ehl humen cehnduct beht th'daioy end heuhrly sao of ehur seuhls f'trehfles? Wot ehem neuh seoinet feh is neither meneh ehr pesition nehr kemfet, bet freelity and fpeuher."

Is that any kind of English for our children to hear? Are we to sit by and let minors absorb this sort of distortion of our mother-tongue and perhaps grow up to speak it themselves? We pay good money to have them taught to say "don't" and "donkey." Are they to be led by outlanders into saying "dehn't" and "dehnkey"? We have been brought up to believe that dropping the final "g" is the mark of a vulgarian. Are our children to hear "nice people" from England saying "runnin' " and "singin' "? No, a theuhsend tehms Neuh!

The fact is that neither Americans nor English have anything to boast of in the matter of pronunciations of their common tongue. There are a few people in each country who have got the hang of it, but for the most part a pretty bad job has been made of the whole thing. Probably the best English is spoken by foreigners who have taken the pains to learn it correctly.

Eight
O'Clock
Sharp

SEVERAL of my young friends (I make friends easily and of all ages) have recently received a questionnaire from the Junior League and the Parents' League designed to bring them to their senses in the matter of tardiness at parties. The idea seems to be that, with people arriving later and later at dinners and dances, the hour of breaking-up is gradually being extended so far into the forenoon of the following day that it cuts in on business conferences and dentist appointments. If guests would arrive at a party on time, they could get it over with and be at home and in the general direction of the bed at a reasonable hour. (If *any* hour can be said to be reasonable.)

Evidently the Junior League and the Parents' League don't care whether I am late to parties or not for they didn't send me a questionnaire. But I am going to answer one anyway, and perhaps from the replies of a man who has been later to more parties than anyone since Charlie Ross (so late, in fact, that many times I have not arrived at all) they may find the solution to their problem.

The first question is: "Are you in favor of dining on time?" This is a little abstruse. There could be no *objection* to dining on time if dinner were served on time, whatever "on time" may mean. Once in a while, especially during the first week after daylight-saving has gone out of effect and I have forgotten to change my watch, I arrive at dinner approximately at the appointed time. What is the result? I am met at the door by a man who hasn't quite finished buttoning his waistcoat and who looks at me with ill-concealed suspicion, the supposition being that anyone arriving so early is either drunk or a reporter. My hat and coat are laid out in solitary state on the hall-catafalque and I am ushered upstairs into the library for half an hour with "The Rise and Fall of Robespierre" and several brisk turns around the room. My host calls from upstairs that he will be "right down" and for me to "make myself at home." This I proceed to do by dropping off into a restless sleep until I am awakened by the tinkling of ice.

The cocktail problem for the guest who has arrived "on time" is no mean one. If you are the first guest to arrive (as you will be if you are "on time") and if you begin drinking cocktails with the first brewing, stringing along with the field as the others arrive, by the time the really late ones have come you are not only the most vivacious guest in the room—you are the host. You do the greeting; you insist on passing the canapés (or what you yourself have left of the canapés exclusive of the powdered egg which has been shed on the rug); you comment on the attire of recent arrivals, and say: "I didn't catch the name" when introduced. In short, you are easily three laps ahead of anyone present except your host (who has been told beforehand by his wife to take it easy) and with your little elfin ways and cute sayings, you endear yourself to one and all and creep into every heart. Thus, before dinner has even commenced, it is your bedtime. This is what comes of arriving at the appointed hour.

Which, in a way, disposes of Question No. 2: "Will you arrive punctually at the hour set?" The answer is "No!"

Question No. 3 is: "Will you get to dances on time?" I am very lucky if I get to dances at all. There is something about the lateness of the hour at which a dance is supposed to begin that makes it rather a nebulous and eerie appointment at best. I can get dressed earlier in the evening with every intention of going to a dance at midnight, but somehow after the theatre the thing to do seems to be either to go to bed or sit around somewhere. It doesn't seem possible that somewhere people can be *expecting* you at an hour like that. Only pixies and banshees have definite midnight appointments, and those are usually on a cabbage-leaf or around the stamen of a blue-bell. Perhaps this vagueness in my mind about dance-dates is a defense mechanism on my part, for I am not a devotee of dancing. Possibly the best way for me to help the Junior League in this particular department of their campaign would be not to *accept* any dance invitations. Then I won't hold things up.

Question No. 4 is: "If you accept a dinner invitation

261

will you really attend?" My answer to this would be: "Well, I will and I won't." It seems like a fair question, however. Somebody has got to know, in order to get the squabs straight, how many people are going to be there, and the best way to find out is to come right out and ask the question point-blank: "If you accept, will you really attend?" My reply, however, is complicated by the fact

that I lose addresses and that a great many people have recently gone in for the unpleasant habit of not having their names in the telephone book. I have spent many a dinner hour, beautifully groomed, standing in a United Cigar store thumbing over the adhesive pages of a telephone directory with no possible way of finding out where I am supposed to be, short of discovering what I did with the little piece of blotting paper on which I originally wrote the address.

Then, too, before I can say definitely whether or not

I will really attend a dinner, I must know about the weather. I am a very poor woodsman, and sometimes great storms come sweeping through the forest which separates my little house from the rest of civilization and I may wander about for weeks before striking the trail. Only last week I started out for a dinner party and, when I was half way through the woods, a driving blizzard came up, trees crashed about me, the winds howled and forced me back and I could not even see the moss on the trees to tell which was north. Naturally, I didn't get to the dinner, but it was a thing which could not have been foreseen. The question, as phrased, is therefore out of order.

The next question is: "Are you in favor of early luncheons?" My reply to this is that I am not in favor of luncheons at all.

This, in a way, clears up my attitude on the subject. I see no way out of the present situation. Parties can not arbitrarily be stopped in time for morning dentist appointments. We aren't living in Russia, you know. The only other course is to have your business and dentist appointments in the afternoon—and that, in turn, will make you late for dinner again. It is a vicious circle, but pleasantly vicious. Let's just let things go on as they are until a general breakdown sets in. That will be plenty of time to stop.

Penguin Psychology*

I T WOULD seem to be a good time for any animals who think themselves highly intelligent to drop into one of our larger colleges and see if there isn't a job there for them. At Columbia University they are crazy for cats who will take intelligence tests; at Yale a good smart monkey can draw down anywhere from $1 to $3 a day, and the Cornell medical college is making very attractive offers for rats to submit themselves to noise tests. An animal with any brains at all is simply a fool not to cash in on the psychological experimenting craze which is sweeping the academic world.

It isn't as if the animals had to be hurt or even fed unpleasant mixtures. The worst that can happen is that you may be frightened by a Cornell professor smashing a paper bag behind your back. The rats who are being used to test the effect of noise on the nervous system may get awfully irritated, what with people rattling things in their ears and blowing whistles, but it is nothing that a good rest over the week-end will not fix up. The cats at Columbia have really nothing to do except step on little disks and open up doors leading to bowls of milk. The life of Reilly was a tough one compared to this. And the Yale monkeys not only are treated just like the other Yale men, but are even taken to Florida dur-

* The interesting scientific experiment referred to in this article was conducted in what is now fondly termed "the bathtub gin era"— a period many now living will recall.—Editor's Note.

264

ing the winter and given a time at Miami. So much attention has not been paid to animals' personal comfort since the time when they were paired off and given that junket on an ark. I am trying to keep the newspaper accounts of these collegiate opportunities from our cat, or she will get dissatisfied with home life and be off to the university to see if some professor can make her jump when he says "Boo!"

I cannot find out just what the college life of these animals is when they are not working in the "lab." Do they live in dormitories together or board around at houses in the town? I suppose that the Yale monkeys go in rather heavily for secret societies and are pretty manly, but the Columbia cats probably go home at night. As the Columbia investigators have found out that alley cats are the smartest of all (one, named Miss Audrey, can practically work a combination on a dial in order to get her bowl of milk) it would be pretty hard to keep them confined in a dormitory after classes. Now, when New Yorkers hear a great disturbance out in back of their apartments, they can lay it to a crowd of "those college cats" and write to the university authorities about it.

It seems, however, as if the academic investigators might find some kinds of animal which would approximate human beings a little more closely than cats and rats. (The Yale monkeys, of course, couldn't be better for the purpose.) I am taking it for granted that the experiments are for the ultimate purpose of applying the principles evolved to human beings and their mental problems. There wouldn't be all this trouble just to pick out the smartest cat on One Hundred and Thirtieth street or the Ithacan rat who could stand the most hooting in his ear. And, since human beings are to be the final beneficiaries of all these experiments, why not take an animal which has more human characteristics than any other next to the monkey—the penguin? I could never understand the almost deliberate ignoring of the penguin in psychological experiments. The penguins themselves, I understand, feel very upset about it.

Any one who has ever watched a penguin will know what I mean. Nowhere in the animal kingdom will you find more human behavior. Slightly drunken human behavior, it is true, but very refined drunkenness. No scenes. No vulgarity. Just the bearing of a rather old colonel in a dinner jacket who had found himself at his club overtaken with a slight giddiness from too much port and is making his way to his cab with all the dignity at his command. If spoken to, he will stop for a second, focus slowly on the obtruder, totter slightly, and then proceed, without so much as a word to indicate that he considers the interruption worthy of his notice. The penguin is the most patrician of all animals who resemble human beings, and it would not be a bad idea to get his consent to a few experiments to be applied to correspondingly patrician members of the human race. Not everybody is going to react. There are still a few gentlemen left in the world, thank Heaven!

I have made a few preliminary experiments with the penguins in the Bronx park zoo, and if Harvard University wants to use them as a basis for a penguin research department it can make the departments of Yale, Columbia and Cornell look pretty silly. I am afraid that Harvard is a little conservative for such advanced research work, however, and I am therefore making a simultaneous offer to the University of Wisconsin. I don't know how the Bronx penguins will feel about taking the trip to Wisconsin, but I should think that if we could get a private train with a club car on it and plenty of Scotch for the journey, they might feel that it was worth their while. They would, of course, be put up at the homes of the faculty during their stay at Madison and would not be expected to attend teas or receptions.

My experiments with the penguins in Bronx park have been superficial but sympathetic. I have taken a book up to the pool around and in which they are accustomed to promenade and have simply engaged them in conversation, just as one gentleman to another. I would not say that they had met me half way, but several of them have accepted cigars (Corona-Coronas) and even a nip if proffered in a tall glass (no ice, please, and plain water), and have eventually condescended to answer a few questions after being assured that there were no reporters present.

One penguin in particular, a Col. MacKenzie of the 12th Penguin Guards, has been extremely gracious, and it is from him that I have collected most of my data. I do not dare take notes while he is talking and so perhaps I have not got the thing exactly as he has said it, but I am sure that I have caught the gist as well as the spirit. He would be furious if he ever knew of this violation of his confidence, but, as he reads nothing but the London *Times*, and occasionally the New York *Herald Tribune*, there is little chance that he will see it. I hope that none of you will be cads enough to go and tell him.

My idea was to discover the scientific effect of prohibition Scotch on brain cells accustomed to the genteel degeneration of the pre-war product (penguins, in their own homes, drink nothing but pre-war liquor), to test the reactions on a highly cultivated and refined mind of vulgar communistic political remarks and to see if penguins, and therefore members of the University or Union League clubs, have a sense of humor.

It took three conferences with Col. MacKenzie to effect my purpose. The first day I pretended to be reading by the pool and did not look up as he tottered by. This evidently intrigued him. I had deliberately taken along a copy of Burke's tirade against the French Revolution and held it so that the colonel could see the title. He stopped in front of me on his third lurch past and stood weaving from side to side trying to catch the name. Very slowly and carefully he took out a pair of nose glasses attached to a long black ribbon which hung across his immaculate shirt front and frankly stared.

"Very sound philosophy this," I said, looking up.

The colonel started to say something, but gave it up to hiccough slightly behind his flapper. He was not accustomed to speaking to strangers. Finally he gave in.

"I see you are a gentleman of the old school," he said, very deliberately and distinctly. "No rubbish. No bolshevism."

"No rubbish, no bolshevism, is my motto, sir," I replied. "I don't know what the world is coming to."

The colonel started to come over and continue the conversation, but slipped ever so little on the wet stone and very nearly fell on his side. This distressed him terribly and he pretended that it was what he had intended to do all along.

"They keep this walk in shocking condition," he said

recovering himself with magnificent dignity. "Shocking condition. The board of governors shall hear of this."

I took out a flask containing some Scotch which I had bought in a drug store on the way up (with a doctor's prescription, of course).

"Could I tempt you, sir?" I asked. Knowing that no penguin would ever drink from a flask I had also brought along two tall glasses and a thermos of plain water. The old gentleman's eyes sparkled as I mixed him a highball. He tucked his glasses away inside his dress waistcoat and came unsteadily nearer.

"An outrage that gentlemen have to drink on the sly like this," he mumbled. "I myself am planning to spend the rest of my life in London. Have relatives there, you know."

I nodded, as if to say that, of course, the whole world knew of the MacKenzies of London, and handed him his glass. He waited until I had made one for myself (very deftly leaving out the Scotch) and raised the glass in military fashion to a point just two inches below his eye.

"The queen, sir!" he said.

"And your very good health, sir," I added.

Col. MacKenzie got his glass to his beak, but no further. The drug store Scotch assailed his patrician nostrils and he could go no further. In order not to hurt my feelings he took a very slight sip and then placed his glass down on the stone beside him. The first part of my experiment had failed miserably. How could I note the effect of prohibition alcohol on a highly sensitized mind if the subject would not drink it?

"New York is not what it used to be," I said sadly, trying another tack.

There was a long silence. I thought that maybe the colonel was offended by my having offered him an inferior grade of liquor. He was weaving slowly in front of me and adjusting his dress tie. An outburst of rage was imminent, I feared. Perhaps an apoplexy. I tossed the contents of my glass into the pool to show him that I, too, had my standards.

"Vile stuff," I said. "I apologize for offering it to you. Now, in the old days, at the Cafe Martin or the Union Club ——"

I caught his eye to see if he was mollified. But, instead, of rage burning there, I saw a film of tears. The old gentleman had broken down at the thought of the dear, dead days, and was on the point of an alcoholic fit of crying. Obviously, I could proceed no further with my tests today.

"Well, I am afraid that I must be going," I said quickly, to cover up his embarrassment. And, bowing deeply, I turned my back to leave.

"Good-by, young man," said the colonel, thickly. "Will you have dinner with me at my club one day? I have some rare old Bourbon. . . . I am most sorry for this display of emotion. . . . The old days, you know . . . the old days." And with a hiccough and a bow deeper than mine which very nearly precipitated him on his head, Col. MacKenzie walked with military unsteadiness down the edge of the pool and joined his clubmates.

So you see I am in a position to get some very valuable scientific data from penguins if Harvard or Michigan is interested. The only trouble will be in keeping the colonel sober enough to react without crying.

Now that you're Tanned---What?

TO THE casual crawler over rocks and beaches in recent summers, if he was at all social-minded, must have come the thought: "To what end all this epidermis-toasting? What is to become of all these sun-tanned backs when winter comes?" The entire Atlantic Coast, from Maine to September, as well as what Mirabeau called *"le bord de la mer"* of the Continent, has been outlined with a fringe of bodies lying prone in the sun patiently awaiting pigmentary alteration. If I were to be given one question on the subject it would be "And for what?"

It isn't as if the process were an easy one to undergo. If you are really going in for tanning every square inch of your body you have got to give yourself over to it as old Simeon Stylites gave himself over to flag-pole sitting. You have got to forswear your friends, your comfort, your meals, and become a tanner. Anyone who has tried to engage a tanner in conversation during this period will realize that he or she might just as well be counted out as far as social intercourse goes. Even if they hear you, they won't answer, either because their mouths are too full of sand or their throats are resting on a rock or simply because they are concentrating so hard on ab-sorbing every one of the sun's rays that they just don't care.

Then, too, there has come into play an added tanning agent in the form of unguents and oils of various kinds.

These have to be applied before getting into the oven and some friend has to be called in to get the stuff well smeared over the small of the back. In places where sand is the geological basis, this process results in a general coating over the calves of the legs and elbows resembling that detected on children's chins in day-coaches after the oranges have been passed around. This coating is not washed off by bathing and has been known to stick until the salad course at dinner that night. There are people who do not mind having small particles of sand on their elbows and the calves of their legs rubbing against their clothing. I, thank God, am not one of these, and none of my people before me have ever been.

As this article is dealing only with the personal discomfort to the tanners themselves, we will say nothing of the trails of oil on the surface of the water left by swimmers who anointed themselves before entering, giving the place the appearance of a cove on the East River at Twenty-third Street. We *would* mention this, however, if we were taking up the effects of tanning on the community in general.

Very well, then. We have seen that a lot of people lie around on their stomachs and hips all summer, with their bathing suits pulled down and up, cut off from their friends, sustaining rock bruises and sand-rash, hurting their eyes and softening the backs of their necks, and all in order to change color on parts of their bodies which, with civilization as petty as it is today, nobody is ever going to see.

Of course, the ladies can display their backs in evening gowns, but, with every woman in the room displaying a brown back, the excitement is somewhat less-

*While they are assembled waiting
for you . . . dash in
dressed in your underclothes*

ened. Even the economist's Theory of Conspicuous Waste will not work in this case, for a brown back is no sign that its owner has had the leisure to acquire it at the shore. She may have got it by fifteen minutes a day under a lamp or by the careful application of powder that very evening. In the early fall social affairs it is the lady with the lily-white shoulders who is the sensation.

But it is the gentlemen who really should begin now to plan what they are going to do in the fall to make up for all the trouble they took during the summer to change color. Aside from a certain pride in showing themselves on the beach and having ladies say, "Honestly, Jimmy, I thought from the back that you were a Negro," theirs must be a short-lived satisfaction. Presumably by September 20 they all have their clothes on again, unless they demonstrate reducing-machines in drugstore windows for a living. At social functions they must appear in formal evening dress, eager to say to the young lady of their choice, "Would you like to see my back?," but prevented by such convention as still remains in polite society. As they look in their mirror each morning and watch the work of an entire summer blushing unseen and gradually fading away without causing even so much as an "O-o-o-h, how *brown* you are!," they are going to begrudge the hours they spent with their mouths in the sand or digging their hips into rocks just to do a Narcissus during the winter.

There are one or two ways in which young gentlemen with left-over tans can make use of them, but I am not sure whether or not they are practical. One would be to go to every dance during the winter dressed as a Greek slave and say, as you enter: "Oh, I thought it was to be fancy-dress!" Then, even if you are put out, a lot of people will have seen you and remarked on how brown you are even though evidently stewed. After going to several dances like this, they may get used to you and let you come in and play around. Another would be to invite guests to your house to dinner and while they are assembled waiting for you to appear, dash in dressed in your underclothes, dashing right out again in simulated confusion, saying: "For Heaven's sake, why don't you let a fellow know you're here!" In case they might not have had time to see your tan, you can trip and fall, taking quite a time to get up. Or perhaps the best way of all would be, no matter where you are, just to say: "I would now like to show you the tan I got last summer" and simply take your clothes off to the point where it isn't funny any more.

Next summer, however, things will probably be different, and we shall see men and women sitting around under great umbrellas with draperies hung over their faces and bodies leaving just holes to see through. It won't make any difference to me either way, as I usually stay indoors during the summer anyway and very seldom take my clothes off in the winter.

Sporting Life in America: Dozing

WE AMERICANS are a hardy race, and hardy races need a lot of sleep. "Sleep, that knits up the ravell'd sleave of care," Shakespeare has called it, and, except for the fact that it doesn't mean much, it is a pretty good simile. I often think of it myself just as I am dropping off into a light doze: "Sleep, that sleeves up the raveled care of . . . knit, that sleeps up the shaveled neeve of pfor—pff—prpf—orpffff' *trailing off into a low whistle*).

One of the most charming manifestations of sleep which we, as a nation, indulge in as a pastime is the Doze. By the Doze I mean those little snatches of sleep which are caught now and then during the day, usually with the collar on and choking slightly, with the head inclined coyly to one side, during which there is a semiconscious attempt to appear as if we were really awake. It is in this department of sleep that we are really at our best.

Of course, there is one form of doze which, to the casual observer or tourist, gives the appearance of legitimate sleep. This is the short doze, or "quickie," which is taken just after the main awakening in the morning. The alarm rings, or the Lord High Chamberlain taps us on the shoulder (in the absence of a chamberlain a relative will do. And right here I would like to offer for examination that type of sadistic relative who takes actual delight in awakening people. They hover about

277

with ghoulish anticipation until the minute arrives when they may legitimately begin their dirty work, and then, leering unpleasantly, they shake the sleeper roughly with a "Come, come! Time to get up!" and wait right there until he is actually out on the cold floor in his bare feet. There is something radically wrong with such people, and the sooner they are exposed as pathological cases the better it will be for the world). I'm sorry. I didn't mean to be nasty about it.

At any rate, we are awakened and look at the clock. There are five minutes before it is absolutely necessary to get out of bed. If we leave shaving until night, there might even be fifteen minutes. If we leave dressing until we get to the office, snatching our clothes from the chair and carrying them downtown on our arm, there might even be half an hour more for a good, health-giving nap. Who knows? Perhaps those few minutes of extra sleep might make us just ten times as efficient during the day! That is what we must think of—efficiency. We must sacrifice our petty opinions on the matter and think of the rest of the day and our efficiency. There is no doubt that fifteen minutes' more sleep would do wonders for us, no matter how little we really want to take it.

By the time we have finished this line of argument we are out pretty fairly cold again, but not so cold that we are not conscious of anyone entering the room. We feel that they are going to say: "Come, come, don't go back to sleep again!" and we forestall this warning with a brisk "I know! I know! I'm just thinking!" This is said with one eye partially open and one tiny corner of the brain functioning. The rest of our powers add up to a total loss.

278

It is one of Nature's wonders how a man can carry on an argument with someone standing beside his bed and still be asleep to all intents and purposes. Not a very good argument, perhaps, and one in which many important words are missing or indistinct, but still an argument. It is an argument, however, which seldom wins, the state of justice in the world being what it is today.

Dozing before arising does not really come within the range of this treatise. What we are concerned with are those little lapses when we are fully dressed, when we fondly believe that no one notices. Riding on a train, for example.

There is the short-distance doze in a day coach, probably the most humiliating form of train sleeping. In this the elbow is rested on the window sill and the head placed in the hand in an attitude of thought. The glass feels very cool on the forehead and we rest it there, more to cool off than anything else. The next thing we know the forehead (carrying the entire head with it) has slid down the length of the slippery pane and we have received a rather nasty bang against the woodwork. They shouldn't keep their glass so slippery. A person is likely to get badly hurt that way.

However, back again goes the forehead against the pane in its original position, with the hand serving more or less as a buffer, until another skid occurs, this time resulting in an angry determination to give the whole thing up entirely and sit up straight in the seat. Some dozers will take four or five slides without whimpering, going back each time for more with apparently undiminished confidence in their ability to see the thing through.

It is a game that you can't beat, however, and the sooner you sit up straight in your seat, the sooner you will stop banging your head.

Dozing in a Pullman chair is not so dangerous, as one does not have the risk of the sliding glass to cope with, but it is even less lovely in its appearance. Here the head is allowed to sink back against the antimacassar—just for a minute to see if the headrest is really as comfortable as it seems. It is then but the work of a minute

for the mouth to open slightly and the head to tip roguishly to the right, and there you are—as pretty a picture as one would care to see. You are very lucky if, when you come to and look about, you do not find your neighbors smiling indulgently at some little vagaries of breathing or eccentricities of facial expression which you have been permitting yourself.

The game in all this public dozing is to act, on awakening, as if you had known all along what you were doing. If your neighbors are smiling, you should smile back, as if to say: "Fooled you that time! You thought I was asleep, didn't you?"

If they are not quite so rude as to smile, but look quickly back at their reading on seeing your eyes open, you should assume a brisk, businesslike expression indicating that you have been thinking out some weighty business problem with your eyes closed, and, now that you have at last come on its solution, that it is snap-snap! back to work for you! If, after a furtive look around, you discover that no one has caught you at it, then it will do no harm to give it another try, this time until your collar chokes you into awakening with a strangling gasp.

The collar, however, is not always an impediment to public dozing. In the theater, for example, a good, stiff dress collar and shirt bosom have been known to hold the sleeper in an upright position when otherwise he might have plunged forward and banged his head on the back of the seat in front.

In my professional capacity as play reviewer I had occasion to experiment in the various ways of sitting up straight and still snatching a few winks of health-giving sleep. I found that by far the safest is to keep one's heavy overcoat on, especially if it is made of some good, substantial material which will hold a sagging torso erect within its folds. With a good overcoat, reënforced by a stiff dress shirt and a high collar, one may even go beyond the dozing stage and sink into a deep, refreshing slumber, and still not be made conspicuous by continual lurchings and plungings. Of course, if you are an uneasy sleeper and given to thrashing about, you will find that even a heavy over-coat will let you down once in a while. But for the average man, who holds approximately the same position after he has gone to sleep, I don't think that this method can go wrong. Its only drawback is that you are likely to get a little warm along about the middle of the second act.

If you don't want to wear your overcoat in the theater, the next best method is to fold the arms across the chest and brace the chin against the dress collar, exerting a slight upward pressure with the arms against the shirt front. This, however, can be used only for the lightest of dozes, as, once unconsciousness has set in, the pressure relaxes and over you go.

Dozing at a play, however refreshing, makes it a bit difficult to follow the argument on the stage, as occasionally the nap drags itself out into a couple of minutes and you awake to find a wholly fresh set of characters on the scene, or even a wholly fresh scene. This is confusing. It is therefore wise to have someone along with you who will alternate watches with you, dozing when you are awake and keeping more or less alert while you are dozing. In this way you can keep abreast of what has been happening.

This, unfortunately, is impossible in personal conversations. If you slip off into a quick coma late some evening when your *vis-à-vis* is telling you about South America or a new solvent process, it is usually pretty difficult to pick up the thread where you dropped it. You may remember that the last words he was saying were "—which is situated at the mouth of the Amazon," but that isn't going to help you much if you come to just as he is asking you: "What would *you* say are?" As in the personal-conversation doze the eyes very seldom completely close (it is more of a turning back of the eyeballs than a closing of the lids) you may escape detection if you have a ready answer for the emergency. I find that "Well, I don't know," said very slowly and deliberately, will fit almost any question that has been asked you. "Yes" and "No" should never be offered, as

they might make you sound even sillier than you look. If you say: "Well, I—don't—know," it will give you a chance to collect your wits (what few there are left) and may lead your questioner into answering the thing himself.

At any rate, it will serve as a stall. If there are other people present, some one of them is quite likely to come to your rescue and say something which will tip you off as to the general subject under discussion. From then on, you will have to fight your own battle. I can't help you.

The whole problem is one which calls for a great deal of thought. If we can develop some way in which a man can doze and still keep from making a monkey of himself, we have removed one of the big obstacles to human happiness in modern civilization. It goes without saying that we don't get enough sleep while we are in bed; so we have got to get a little now and then while we are at work or at play. If we can find some way to keep the head up straight, the mouth closed, and just enough of the brain working to answer questions, we have got the thing solved right there.

I am working on it right now, as a matter of fact, but I find it a little difficult to keep awake.

The Bathroom Revolution

A FIRM of what purport to be plumbers (but whom I suspect of being royalist propagandists trying to get the Bourbon kings back into power again) once issued a catalogue showing how to make your bathroom look like the Great Hall at Versailles—or I guess the best way to go about it would be to make the Great Hall at Versailles look like a bathroom. No one would have a room that size in his house to start with. And, as an old bathroom lover, I resent the tone of this pamphlet.

According to these so-called "plumbers," they will come trooping into your new house—it would have to be a new house, for you never could get it into your old one—and will install there a "Diocletian bath" (page 4 of the catalogue) which, judging from the colored illustration, is a room about the size of the tapestry room in the Metropolitan Museum of Art. It has a sunken bathtub, and great mirrors stretch from floor to ceiling, while over a Roman bench is draped a blue robe suitable for wrapping up an emperor in.

Or, for milady, there is the "Trianon bath" (page 5) which resembles one of those French interiors we used to see in the old Biograph pictures when the movies were young. The bathtub in the "Trianon" arrangement is so cleverly concealed that a person might go pattering about with his towel for days among the silk hangings and rococo furniture without ever finding it at all.

On page 7 we have the "Récamier bath," which is

evidently intended for formal minuet parties and possibly a royal levee during the season, but which bears no resemblance to what used to be known as "the bathroom" in old-fashioned houses of the 1920-'29 period.

The "Petti Palace bath" and the "Flamingo bath," on pages 8 and 9, I will not attempt to describe, as you would not believe me. Suffice it to say that the "Petti Palace" bathtub could be used either for bathing in large groups or for small naval engagements between ships of the third class.

Now this elaboration of the bathroom is all very well in its way, provided it does not make us effete as a nation and does not get us into other old Roman customs of lolling about on couches at our meals and holding bunches of grapes up over our heads, but, since a revolution in bathrooms is evidently well on its way, let up hope that too much will not be sacrificed to magnificence and that taking a bath will be made such a formal ritual that it can be indulged in only by those who can trace their ancestry back to the Merovingian kings and have inherited robes of silk and gold to dress the part in. I know very well that my old blue toweling bathrobe would never fit in with any room shown in this catalogue. Rather than enter one of them in my straw slippers and flannel pajamas I would just take a quick sponge bath in my own room and let it go at that.

In the first place, it would be hard to heat one of these great halls, and a bathroom which is not piping hot had better be used to store trunks in. The only way that I can see to get the "Diocletian bath" fit for human occupancy on a cold winter's morning would be to have

*My old blue towelling bathrobe would never fit in with any room
shown in this catalogue*

an army of serfs dragging in monster logs and piling them in a blazing heap in a fireplace right beside the tub. And who wants an army of serfs popping in and out of the bathroom when he is bathing? It is difficult enough as it is now to make people keep the bathroom door shut on a cold morning, without bringing in a lot of strangers.

And, even with a huge fire blazing, the only part of you to be kept warm would be the side toward the fireplace, and what good will it do you to have 10-foot mirrors lining the walls of your bathroom, if, when you get out of your bath, you are going to have to look at yourself turning blue under your very eyes? I am not crazy about the mirror idea, anyway, even in summer. I would prefer to forget, if possible.

The only advantage that I can see to the ballroom-size bathroom on a cold morning (provided some way can be found to heat it) would be that one would have more space in which to dress. In the old-fashioned 10-by-12 bathroom there is always a little difficulty in finding a place to put one's clothes after the mad dash from the cold bedroom with an armful of the day's garments.

Of course, some of the smarter ones undress in the bathroom the night before and have time to leave their clothing in neat piles where it can be easily reached the next morning, but even this foresight does not cover the getting of clean shirts out of the bureau (a process at which several people already have frozen to death this winter) or the problem of keeping the trousers in press overnight. You can't expect trousers to look like much after they have been draped over a bathtub or left hanging from the medicine closet door all night.

In the "Petti Palace bath," I must admit, there is room for a complete wardrobe in which a dozen suits may be hung and a row of bureaus containing enough clean shirts and under-garments to last the winter. In fact, if you had the "Petti Palace bath" in your house you could rent the rest of the rooms out to lodgers and just live in there (and the adjoining bedroom) until spring came.

One big item which is likely to be overlooked in these monster bathrooms, however, is the upkeep. The week they are installed they may be impressive, but it would take a corps of interior decorators to keep them so, especially if there are children in the family. In a house where there are small children the bathroom soon takes on the appearance of the Old Curiosity Shop. In even one small bathroom, when there are children in the house, one finds rocking horses, milk heaters, tin soldiers, enormous rubber ducks, odd books, overshoes, and skates, and, once in a while, reefers and stocking caps belonging to neighbors' children. Sometimes even the neighbors' children themselves.

Can you imagine what would happen in the "Flamingo bath" with its great stretches of red lacquer tiling if a family of children were given the run of it? A man with some idea of taking a bath would have to climb over miles of electric train tracks and under railroad switches. He most likely would have to cope with submarines and rubber whales in the tank-like tub and would be lucky if he got out without a nasty fall on a slippery floor which had been prepared, and used, as a skating rink. Instead of a stray tin soldier now and then, he would probably step on a complete brigade of bayonets, the bath mat being temporarily used as a tent with an American flag flying from it.

Of course, it may be argued, a house with room enough in it for a "Flamingo bath" would also be likely to contain a nursery, but, unless children have changed a lot in the last two or three days, they prefer the bathroom to the nursery any day as a scene for their activities. And, unless parents have changed a lot in the same space of time, what the children want, they get.

The grownups, too, would contribute to the chaos of the décor. How long would the "Récamier bath" look like Mme. Récamier after daddy had changed his razor blades six or seven times and had used up all but a third each of five tubes of tooth paste? There seems to be a common strain of miserliness in the American people when it comes to throwing away tooth paste tubes which have a little left in the bottom. I have seen bathroom shelves piled high with two-thirds used tubes (all without caps), and a bottle of mouth wash, with maybe an eighth of an inch of liquid showing, has been known to keep its place beside a fresh bottle until the fresh bottle is down to an eighth of an inch and, in turn, takes its place beside a new one. It is only when the door of the medicine closet refuses to shut, or the whole shelf-ful of old aluminum topples over into the wash basin that a general cleaning out is instigated. (I am not speaking of my own bathroom shelf. That is kept very neat. I refer to the bathroom shelves in other houses.)

Just as a detail, but one which is quite important to a successful bathroom regime, I should like to know what provision is made in these luxurious and sensual bath palaces for such minor items as the recovery of lost tooth paste tube caps. If they have solved this problem, they may justify themselves. The fact that so many capless tubes are seen lying about in people's bathrooms is due to the fact that the caps are, at that moment, lodged in the spout of the wash basin. I don't know what the capacity of the average spout for tube caps is, but I know, by actual count, that there are nine in mine

right now. I used to claw them up after they had slipped out of my hand and gone down the vent. I could see them peeking up at me, just about a quarter of an inch below the rim, and have sometimes spent 15 or 20 minutes trying to hook them out with a tooth brush or razor blade (razor blades are not to be recommended as tube cap hooks, however, owing to the danger of leaving a piece of finger in the spout with the cap).

But I am older now, and more cynical, and, after the first frantic manoeuvres to catch the cap before it rolls out of sight, I give the whole thing up and go on calmly brushing my teeth. I have other things to do. But it does seem as if these royalist plumbers who have gone to such lengths to make the bathroom a menace to our homespun civilization at least might have worked out some way of avoiding this common catastrophe.

Just one more word about the menace of these patrician pools. What will be their logical effect on guest towels? If, in our modest little white-tiled bathrooms, it has been necessary to make the guest towel a semi-rigid, highly glazed bit of vivid tapestry in order to impress the guests, what will have to be done to make it show up in a room which is already a treasure chamber of bijouterie and a royal riot of color? The ordinary towels for family use will have to be at least as elaborate and showy as guest towels are today. What is there left in magnificence for guest toweling? Nothing, that I can see, but spun gold with ermine fringes, or perhaps small sheets of strung jewels glittering in the light of a concealed and highly colored bulb. Well, no one will ever use them anyway, any more than they do today.

If I ever to succumb to the Louis XIV instinct in me (and make enough money) and do have one of the "Diocletian baths" installed in that great big new house I shall build, there will be a secret door, hidden behind a rare tapestry, to which I alone will have the key. Behind it I will have built a nice, small, warm, white-tiled bathroom, with good brown coarse towels and a sponge, and a tub into which I can get and read with comfort. Any kings or princes or motion-picture actors that I have out for the week-end may use the other.

"What Shall We Say?"

I DON'T want to be an alarmist—oh, what do I care? Sure, I'll *be* an alarmist, and will point out that the more literate sections of our country are today on the verge of an epidemic of brain-fag which threatens to plunge us into a national mental collapse.*

"What!" you will say. "An epidemic of brain-fag which threatens to plunge us into a national mental collapse? Man, you are mad!" I will show you how mad I am.

Go into any telegraph office in any one of our larger cities and, at three out of the six desks reserved for customers (two of which are equipped with chained pencils, one of which has a point), you will see people sitting with their heads in their hands obviously going through a critical period of mental *accouchement*. They write out messages, tear them up, gnaw at their knuckles, write out more messages and tear them up. Perhaps there will be two or three grouped about one desk, each one making occasional feverish suggestions which seem to die on their lips with the uttering. The atmosphere is one of complete human frustration and the very air vibrates with mental waves beating themselves out against the walls.

These people are trying to compose original and

* Since this telling article was written, circumstances have removed the threat to our national well-being that so justifiably aroused Mr. Benchley's concern.—Editor's Note.

294

funny telegrams to their friends. They are breathlessly trying to keep up with a movement which has gained such force in the past few years as to oppress even the casual sender of wires and to sweep the pioneer wags who started it over the hill to the madhouse. About the only citizens who can go right into a telegraph office, write out their messages, and turn them in without losing great handfuls of hair in their composition are those who are sending messages of condolence, and it won't be long before some comic starts the fashion of making even these facetious, probably with one to the bereaved reading: "What are you doing day after to-morrow?"

A little group of merrymakers get together for dinner and, along about the potato-chip course, someone suggests: "We ought to send a wire to Eddie!" This seems a bully idea at the time. Eddie would so love to be there, and will get such a good laugh out of a kidding telegram from his old pals. They laugh just to think of how Eddie will laugh. So a telegraph pad is sent for, and someone who has a pencil starts out by writing Eddie's name and address in very large, plain letters at the top.

"What shall we say?"

At this point, the dinner is abandoned, all digestive processes are halted in mid-air, and the gay little group settles down to the serious business of thinking up a funny telegram for Eddie.

No one wants to start suggesting, for fear that his suggestions won't be funny enough. The man with the pencil writes out something tentatively, but decides before submitting it that it won't do. So he tears up that blank and writes Eddie's name and address again.

"How about saying: 'Have just found a piece of food in the dinner. What shall we do?',," someone suggests faintly.

Several of the more polite ones laugh without feeling, but no move is made to write it down. Its sponsor blushes and retires.

"How about this?" (a fatal prelude to any suggestion): "'Cross marks our room. Wish you were here.'"

Not even the polite ones laugh at this. It is withdrawn

hastily. There is a long silence. The man with the pencil has been making another stab at it by himself, and proceeds to read off what he has written:

"'Don't let any ——' No, I guess that isn't very funny." And he tears up the blank in embarrassment.

Deep depression settles over the group and the clock ticks gloomily. Everyone is trying to think of something comical and everyone is rapidly losing caste with himself and with the rest of the party. What once was a bright little extemporaneous dinner has solidified into a Regents' examination period. The whole thing finally breaks up by sending a wire to Eddie reading: "HOW ARE YOU KID?," with nobody satisfied, including Eddie, who doesn't know whom it is from.

This dispiriting procedure is repeated, either in groups or singly, every time anyone sails for Europe, takes a train to California (catching the traveller at Albany, Rochester, Chicago, and Albuquerque with telegrams of progressive hilarity is an art so fine as to be practically extinct), or, for those whose acquaintance includes mimes and mountebanks, every time a new play opens.

Telegrams to opening nights are in a class by themselves. They must be good, because they are likely to be displayed on the dressing-room mirror of the recipient during the run of the play. They must be different, because these people check up. And they must be frequent, as the average life of a play today is four hours. The whole thing has become a nightmare.

Thus we find that not only is the national brain-fibre rapidly wearing itself out, but most of the fun of dining, travelling, and opening is being dimmed by the constant obligation of being funny about it in ten words. My suggestion would be that the Western Union add to its collection of readymade greetings for Christmas, Easter, Yom Kippur, and Childbirth a printed form including twenty excruciating telegrams to be sent "just for the fun of it," and twenty even more excruciating ones to be sent in reply.

Either this, or begin all over again and go back to the old way of just saying: "Bon Voyage," "Good Luck," or, better yet, sending no telegram at all.

A Vanishing Art

SOMEHOW I have a feeling that, no matter how far out of work I may be, I shall never be able to make my living by putting little ships into glass bottles. There must be some people who do, for one is constantly seeing bottled ships in store windows. I never could quite figure out just what kind of store it was that would feature a ship in a bottle as a window display, but as there is usually an 18th-century highboy and a pair of bellows alongside the bottle, it can't be one of the more essential emporia. I guess that you would just call it a "ship-in-bottle store."

However, the fact that putting little ships into bottles is not a useful trade is not the reason why I would not go in for it. Look at what I am doing now! No, the reason for my eschewing that form of gainful activity is simply that I haven't the slightest idea how it is done. And I doubt if I ever could learn.

I have often tried to figure it out while standing, on a busy day in my own trade, in front of a ship-in-bottle store. Is it possible that the tiny ship is made and rigged and set up and then the glass blown around it? Blowing glass in itself is enough of a mystery to me without having it complicated by having to blow it around a ship. I rather doubt if that is the way the thing is done.

The only other solution is that the bottle is already blown and the ship is made inside the bottle. This, too, sounds implausible. Some sort of man or woman (or very dexterous child) has got to make the ship, and you can't tell me that any one, no matter how small, can get right inside one of those bottles and build a ship. I may get a funny, vacant look in my eyes once in a while, and I may not be very good at adding up my check stubs, but I'm no fool. Nobody makes those ships from the inside out.

This leaves what? Nothing! Either the ship is made first or the bottle is made first. The hole in the neck of the bottle is not large enough to allow for a full-rigged ship being let down through it. You can tell that at a glance. There is nothing left except for the ponderer to go crazy. I have tried that, too.

I once tracked a ship-in-bottle putter to his workshop and tried to find out how he worked it. I was spending the summer on the Atlantic coast (sometimes here and sometimes there, mostly a compromise between the two) and in an old Cape Cod antique shop I saw one of the accursed things. I went into the shop and asked the old lady (don't let her know I called her an "old lady," please) who had made it. She, with that old New England cordiality which has made that section of the country the flourishing centre it now is, left the room without answering me. But I found out from a customer (a summer resident who came from Wisconsin) that a gentleman who lived in the white house down by the steamship dock had wrought this wonder. So I set out in search of him.

His name was Capt. Whipple and he was 167 years old, although he lied about his age and claimed to be only 160.

"Cap'n," I said (from now on I shall spell the title

"Captain," but you must remember that what I really said was "Cap'n") , "Captain, how in (naming a certain flower) do you put those little ships into those bottles?" A fair question, and deserving of a fair answer.

The captain whittled a piece from his calloused thumb and spat reflectively. "Wal," he said (from now on I shall spell the words as they should be spelled, without reference to the Cape Cod pronunciation), "Well, it's a long story."

Going back to my hotel and getting a chair, I drew it up beside the old gentleman, all attention.

"Shoot, kid!" I said.

The seafaring man took the stub of a pencil and began figuring on the back of the original of a letter from Thomas Jefferson to Martha Custis (a little scandal which has never come to light, but which, while it lasted, was a peach). Then he looked up at me with his little, watery blue eyes aglint.

"You're from New York, ain't you?" he asked.

I blushed prettily.

"It will cost you just $500 to know," he said. "And, at that, I am cheating myself."

I thought it over. Five hundred dollars to learn how to put a ship in a bottle, when the chances were that I never would be called upon to put anything into a bottle, much less a ship. And even if, at some time or other, I should be faced with the necessity, I could always plead a headache or the fact that I had no ship with me at the moment. So I took an old Revolutionary cradle which was standing nearby and placed it firmly over the old gentleman's head until nothing was visible of him above his shoulders. On this I piled several pewter candlesticks, a spinning wheel, and a portrait of Gen. Howe. This done, I left the ancient mariner and artisan with his secret.

The main trouble, however, with taking up ship-in-bottle putting as a trade (aside from the difficulty of finding out how it is done) would seem to be that it doesn't offer much opportunity for advancement to a young man. You can't get ahead very fast. Suppose you do learn how to do it and serve an apprenticeship to some expert ship-in-bottle putter for five years. You are then promoted to head of the bottling department. What is there left? You are as far as you can go, unless you start in for yourself. And I should imagine that the consumer demand for ships in bottles would be soon exhausted in any one community, with very little turnover.

One is reminded (and, let us be quite frank about it, when I say "one is reminded" I mean "I am reminded") * of the business troubles of the man who polished the commemorative brass cannon in Ypsilanti, Mich. (I have always heard that it was Ypsilanti, Mich., but I am willing to retract if it is not true.) It seems that the residents of Ypsilanti, Mich., shortly after the Civil War decided that some sort of monument or *denkmal* should be placed in a public square to remind future generations of Michigan's part in the great struggle. So a large brass commemorative cannon was placed on the common (if there is a common in Ypsilanti) and a veteran of the war was engaged, at a nominal salary, to keep this cannon in good condition. He was to polish it

*The author is indebted to Mr. "Terry" McGovern of Cornell University for the following business fable.

twice a week and see that small boys did not hide in it. Aside from this, his time was his own.

This business routine went on for 25 years. The veteran was faithful at his task of polishing the commemorative brass cannon and its splendor and shining surface were the admiration of every one who visited Ypsilanti, Mich., during those 25 years, to say nothing of the natives. "The commemorative brass cannon of Ypsilanti, Mich.," became a byword throughout the state for expressing how shiny a commemorative brass cannon could be made.

One evening, during the veteran's 26th year of service, he came home to supper at his usual hour (4:30), but his wife noticed that he was more depressed than was his wont. He hardly touched his food, and sat in moody contemplation of the backs of his polish-stained hands. His wife was worried.

"What is it, Joe?" she asked. "What is the matter?"

"Oh, nothing, my dear," said her husband, and turned in a brave attempt to finish his cutlet.

"Come, come," said the companion of his 25 years of labor (he had married immediately on getting the job of polishing the commemorative brass cannon) , "I know that something is wrong. You are depressed."

The gray-haired man put down his knife and looked his wife in the eye.

"You're right," he said, as he took her hand in his. "I am depressed. Things haven't been going very well down at the cannon lately."

"You don't mean that you're fired, Joe!" she said, fearfully.

"No, no! Never fear about that," was his reply. "They couldn't fire me. I know too much. They would be afraid that I might make trouble. But I am discouraged about my work. I don't seem to be getting ahead. For 25 years I have been polishing that cannon and putting everything that I had into making it bright and shiny. I have done my job well—no one can deny that. But recently I have got to thinking. What is it leading to? Where am I getting? Where is the future in polishing commemorative brass cannons?" And the old man broke down and cried.

His wife was silent for a minute. Then she stroked his head and said: "I know, Joe. I have worried a little myself. And I have figured it out this way. In the last 25 years we have saved a little money. I have put aside a dollar here and a dollar there when you didn't know about it. We have quite a tidy little nest egg in the bank now, and here is my suggestion: Let's take that money, buy a cannon, and go into business for ourselves!"

Such, I should think, would be the problem which would confront every middle-aged man who finds himself, at the age of 55, a putter-in-bottles of little ships. What is the future of such work? Even if he goes into business for himself like the polisher of the commemorative brass cannon of Ypsilanti, Mich., how can he meet competition? Of course, he can vary the types of ships he puts into the bottles. The old, square-rigged merchantman having gone out of date, he could put in models of the *Bremen* or destroyers, but, with all this

303

talk of naval reduction going on, dealing in battleships and destroyers is a pretty precarious business.*

England pleads that her navy has been more than an engine of war during the last two centuries, that it has been a career for the finest of her young men. She naturally recoils from any proposition which would eliminate such patrician employment. But what about those unfortunates who find themselves with no models for bottle-putting? These artisans must either stick to the old clipper ships which their grandfathers put in bottles, or put in battleships which may be, in a few years, against the law. Of course, they could begin putting in models of reapers and binders, or of printing presses, or any of the other thousand-and-two engines of peace, but that really wouldn't be right. It has got to be a ship if the old tradition is to be maintained.

And so, to all young men who are going out into the world to make their living, I would say: "Think twice before you go in for putting little ships in bottles. That is, unless you are planning to spend a lot of your time in jail, where time hangs heavy."

I suppose that I shall get a lot of indignant letters from the trade for issuing this advice. But it comes from the heart.

* This article was obviously written on the eve of that benighted era when nations were busily engaged in sinking not each other's ships, as the custom is today, but—oddly enough—their own.—Editor's Note.